The Brain-Based Classroom
Practical Guide

Also by
Kieran O'Mahony, PhD FRGS

The Brain-Based Classroom:
Accessing Every Child's Potential Through Educational Neuroscience
(Routledge, 2021)

Brain-centric Design:
The Surprising Neuroscience Behind Learning with Deep Understanding
(Thanet House Publishing, 2019) with co-author Rich Carr, BcID

Mediated Pedagogy in a Blended Environment:
Chapter in Ecojustice, Citizen Science & Youth Activism (Springer, 2015)

Connecting Formal and Informal Learning Experiences:
That Dam Project (Proquest, 2010)

Waldseemuller World Map 1507
(Educare Press, 2003)

Geography and Education:
Through The Souls of Our Feet
(Educare Press, 2001)

Dictionary of Geographical Literacy:
The Complete Geographical Reference
(Educare Press, 1993)

Geographical Literacy:
What Every American Should Know About Geography—and More
(Educare Press, 1991)

I have been teaching for 14 years, and I have never received a training that completely changed my mindset until now. This conference has meant the world to me. Teaching with the brain in mind will help us meet the needs of each student in our classroom. The information from the work of the Neural Education group can quite literally change the lives of everyone it touches. I have taken away knowledge from this conference that will help me adjust my instruction in the classroom, my work with other educators, how I parent, and how I communicate with my family and community. Best training ever!!!

- Lori Donati, Reading Specialist - Sawyer Woods Elementary

I have devoted my career (15 years) to helping students grow as learners. During my tenure, I have witnessed limited success with different waves of educational reform. As soon as I found Neural Education, things clicked - I was able to connect with my students through the lens of neuroscience to have a real impact on learning and social emotional development. With this new perspective, I started my own school - The Seattle School for Boys - we put Neural Education practices and methods into action to create an equitable learning space where boys can develop empathy, compassion and a sense of identity.

- Jerome Hunter - Seattle School for Boys

By understanding the brain and how we react to our environment, I now have a new and amazing perspective as an educator on how we can connect with all of our students, regardless of their life trauma, so they can be successful, not only in the classroom, but for the rest of their lives.

- Leah Sandlian - High School PE/Health Teacher, Fife School District

In my twenty-five years of being in education, Neural Ed is **HANDS DOWN** the **VERY BEST** professional development I've been part of ... ever!!

- Karey Richardson - Assistant Principal, Puyallup SD

I am confident that this neural ed approach will add value to learning outcomes for children in schools across America and ... across Africa.

- Prof. Tabitha - Wang'eri, Kenyatta University, Kenya

The Brain-Based Classroom
Practical Guide

Kieran O'Mahony

Brain-Based Solutions
Seattle, WA
An Educare Press Book

Copyright © 2023 Kieran O'Mahony

All rights reserved. No part of this work may be reproduced or used in any manner without written permission of the copyright owner except for the use of children practicing art or reading.

For information about this title or to order other books and/or electronic media, contact the publisher:
Publisher: Brain-Based Solutions, Seattle, WA.
Email: Kieran@brainbasedsolutions.org
https://brainbasedsolutions.org

Teacher Practical Guide for implementing Neuroscience of Learning Series: Tiger Schmiger™ Books for Teachers and Children Only.

Names: O'Mahony, Kieran, 1953- author.

Title: The brain-based classroom practical guide / Kieran O'Mahony.

Description: First printing 2023. | Seattle, WA : Brain-Based Solutions, [2023] | Series: Tiger Schmiger books for teachers and children only. | "An Educare Press book." | "Teacher practical guide for implementing neuroscience of learning"--Title page verso. | Includes bibliographical references and index.

Identifiers: ISBN: 978-0-944638-70-5 (Spiral) | 978-0-944638-72-9 (Flip Book) | 978-0-944638-54-5 (Paper) | 978-0-944638-76-7 (Spanish) | 978-0-944638-71-2 (E-Book) | 978-0-944638-75-0 (Audio)

Subjects: LCSH: Learning, Psychology of. | Teaching--Psychological aspects. | Cognitive learning theory. | Cognitive neuroscience. | Cognitive science. | Neuropsychology. | Learning strategies. | Behavior modification. | Teaching--Methodology. | Teaching--Aids and devices.
| BISAC: EDUCATION / Educational Psychology. | EDUCATION / Special Education / General.
| EDUCATION / Teaching / Methods & Strategies.

Classification: LCC: LB1062 .O53 2023 | DDC: 370.15/23--dc23

Book Production by NoShooz Publishing, , Inc. Bainbridge Island, WA.

Dedication

to Neural Education Champions, who are breaking the mold...
teaching in a remarkably different way

*A man who carries a cat by the tail
learns something he can learn in no other way*

— Mark Twain

Contents

Acknowledgments xvii

Preface: Dear Reader… xxiii

Introduction: Ms. Pedersen's Story xxvii

Section I: Regulate 1

01. Problem: School Sucks! 8
    Solution: The Mindset Continuum - Intelligence 9

02. Problem: I'm No Good at… 10
    Solution: The Mindset Continuum - Talent 11

03. Problem: Avoid Challenges 12
    Solution: The Mindset Continuum - Challenges 13

04. Problem: Give up Easily 14
    Solution: The Mindset Continuum: Persistence 15

05. Problem: Effort is Fruitless 16
    Solution: The Mindset Continuum - Effort 17

06. Problem: Ignore Useful Negative Criticism 18
    Solution: The Mindset Continuum - Criticism 19

07. Problem: Threatened by Success of Others 20
    Solution: The Mindset Continuum - Success of Others 21

08. Problem: Plateau Early, Fail to Reach Potential 22
    Solution: The Complete Mindset Continuum 23

09. Problem: Deterministic Worldview 24
    Solution: Greater Sense of Personal Freedom 25

10. Problem: Asking Questions Won't Work 26
    Solution: Predictable, Consistent & Kind 27

11. Problem: Scaffolds can be Ineffective 28
    Solution: Scaffolds can be Amazing 29

12. Problem: Dysfunction 30
    Solution: The Rhythmic Envelope 31

13. Problem: Stuck With the Contagious 3 P's 32
    Solution: Get Unstuck From the Contagious 3 P's 33

14. Problem: Calm Down! 34
    Solution: Are You OK? 35

15. Problem: The Perils of Punishment 36
    Solution: All the Children Get All the Joy 37

16. Problem: I'm Angry 38
    Solution: What's Below Anger 39

17. Problem: Behavior Is… 40
    Solution: Communication 41

18. Problem: 2 x 4 42
    Solution: 2 x 10 43

Section II: Relate 45

19. Problem: Invisible Plan 48
    Solution: I Wish My Teacher Knew… 49

20. Problem: Screaming & Kicking 50
    Solution: Transitions can be Predictable 51

21. Problem: Threats Stop Learning 52
    Solution: Sense of Belonging Enhances Learning 53

22. Problem: Can't Breathe 54
    Solution: Relate with Jewelry 55

23. Problem: Can't Think 56
    Solution: Mirror with Peer 57

24. Problem: Dandelinic Compliance 58
    Solution: Orchidial Chaos 59

25. Problem: Managing Classrooms 60
    Solution: Managing Brains 61

26. Problem: Teacher Shouldn't Be Busy 62
    Solution: Children Should Be Busy 63

27. Problem: Reminder Oops! 64
    Solution: Morning Journey with Hippocampus 65

28. Problem: Judgmental Cat & Mouse 66
    Solution: Be Curious! 67

29. Problem: Child needs Help 68
    Solution: Simplify Rubrics 69

30. Problem: Time Out/Calm Down Corner 70
    Solution: All I Need to Know… 71

31. Problem: Neural Diversity 72
    Solution: Presume Competence 73

32. Problem: Children Have No Energy 74
    Solution: Belly Breathe 75

33. Problem: I'm Bored 76
    Solution: Brilliant Bored Brain 77

34. Problem: Child-Centric? 78
    Solution: Appetite Over Aptitude 79

Section III: Reason 81

35. Problem: Persistence of Misconceptions 84
    Solution: Disequilibrium 85

36. Problem: I'm Lost 86
    Solution: Mastering Mastery 87

37. Problem: Right or Wrong 88
    Solution: Multiple Perspectives 89

38. Problem: Inert Scraps Take Up Space 90
    Solution: Reflect Collects Your Thoughts 91

39. Problem: Rote Memorization is Real 92
    Solution: Revised Thinking is Magic 93

40. Problem: Limping Alone in Tall Grass 94
    Solution: Middle of the Herd Report Out 95

41. Problem: No We Didn't… 96
    Solution: Long Lasting Connections 97

42. Problem: Tiered Systems 98
    Solution: A Child's Brain 99

43. Problem: Autonomic Nervous System Reactivity 100
    Solution: School-Friendly Genetics 101

44. Problem: Negative Priming 102
    Solution: RAS-ify Your Children 103

45. Problem: If…Then Mistake 104
    Solution: No Strings Attached 105

46. Problem: Cortisol Effect 106
    Solution: Ball Drop 107

47. Problem: What's the Big Idea? 108
    Solution: Consolidate the Big Idea with LTP 109

48. Problem: Left in the Dust 110
    Solution: LTP Strengthens Working Memory 111

49. Problem: Cognitive Load 112
    Solution: From Automaticity to Cognitive Load 113

50. Problem: Imposter Syndrome 114
    Solution: Purposeful Mastery 115

51. Problem: Learned Helplessness 116
    Solution: Expected Confidence 117

52. Problem: No Brain 118
    Solution: Whole Brain 119

53. Problem: Pedagogy 120
    Solution: A Pedagogic Model 121

54. Problem: The Phenotype Child 122
    Solution: Regulation for Reason 123

55. Problem: I Need Proof 124
    Solution: Circuit Synchrony 125

56. Problem: Words Count 126
    Solution: Focus 127

57. Problem: Memory is Fallible 128
    Solution: Play for Memory 129

58. Problem: Mental Models for UDL 130
    Solution: Greenhouse 131

59. Problem: Fear of Math 132
    Solution: Deep Learning 133

60. Problem: Deliberate Behavior in Social Gatherings 134
    Solution: Involuntary Reaction Drives Behavior 134

Epilogue 139
Glossary 147
Index 177

Acknowledgments

We stand on the shoulders of those who have gone before us and were kind enough to write things down. I am particularly grateful for opportunities to carry out research projects and interventions in classrooms of all ages and in places as distant as Ireland, Africa, Australia, New Zealand, India, China and the United States. The brain is the same no matter the geography.

The Brain-Based Classroom that this Practical Guide is meant to accompany, was commissioned by Taylor & Francis Group (London and New York, 2021) and had to be an overly academic undertaking to fulfill requirements relating to the Routledge academic series - An **Eye on Education** Book. As a result, there was not a lot of energy or content dedicated to the implementation of the many pedagogical dictates that were envisioned by a neural education approach to classroom teaching and learning. Strategies, constructs and commitments that were implied in that earlier work, needed to be made visible in hands-on classes with early adopters and practitioners who were convinced that the ideas had merit and demanded rigor. This Practical Guide is an attempt to bring that rigor to implementation. It is designed to be flexible enough so that a teacher in a classroom anywhere can adapt it to the needs of the situation and the audience being served.

I am grateful to the many educators who walked with me in the careful outlining and structuring of these practices, processes and strategies. Practices are routines and verbiage that educators use day-to-day in the performance of their profession. Processes are localized interpretations of systemic and regulatory activation of learning spaces in usually large, unwieldy and complex undertakings for millions of children every day. And strategies are thinking systems and mental models that emerge from charged, revolutionary vocabularies that include the latest findings from laboratories across the world in neuroscience and learning sciences.

Foremost among these educators are the certified champions in Neural Education and leaders that help greenhouse and support each other week over week and month after month. In this amazing greenhouse community we find that where sensitive orchid brains flourish, our resilient dandelion partners thrive just as well. New discoveries are made visible every time we meet. For that, and for their dedicated perseverance and commitment, I am very thankful. Every time we witness a child find voice and give sustenance to another learner, we are reminded that the teaching profession is the most valuable and rewarding expression of neural potential on the planet.

I'm especially indebted to the weekly Neural Ed team who tirelessly commit to building structures and programs, which, over time, advance the field with emerging methodologies that have come into play over the past decade. Thank you to Missy Widmann, Mary Snyder, Tabitha Ellison, Allison Abrahmse, Terri Farrar, and Sophia Monge. Champions are not only changing the face of education in their classrooms every day, they are carefully gathering data, writing about their experiences and sharing their work with colleagues and other educators wherever they can get an opportunity and exposure.

In particular, I appreciate the genius and attention to detail that an early adapter and a stalwart champion, Tabitha Ellison, offered in the first reading of this manuscript in preparation. The work is improved in its focus, delivery and connection to the classroom because of her expertise. I learn so much from our fabulous educators each time we talk. Thanks and gratitude to Nora Zollweg for a genius strategy regarding regulation with recycled jewelry - small motor and cognitive load that works with ease and grace.

To be a partner to incredible teaching showcases is an experience to be cherished and an honor to witness. As team players in course delivery during Summer Institutes, where thousands of new teachers cut their teeth in this groundbreaking direction in a changed post-pandemic learning space, is truly mind-blowing and riveting. Pacific Lutheran University campus faculty and staff are unfaltering compatriots on this journey, which illuminate a neural lens in learning spaces.

Highest accolades and heartiest appreciation for the amazing individuals, friends, colleagues and educators who are first in line for championing this work to educators worldwide. Thank you to Gunner Argo, Audrey Gallagher, Dani Hylton, Mary Catherine Pilon, Wendy Beldin, Terri Farrar, Kristyn Dahl, Dawn Pringle, Rachel Collier, Laurie Donati, Taylor Cassidy, Paige Wescott, Megan Bublitz, Darcy Dickerman, Terri Ann Schiferl, Jerome Hunter, Valli Rebsamen, and Gaudencio Merafuentes.

On the frontlines, there are countless other individuals who experienced the spark of engagement through a neural lens and are implementing cognitive mental models in their homes and schools as they can. I wish to acknowledge the multiplicative interchange and impact for millions of children because of their decision to embrace and engage. I would like to reach out to every part of the United States and Canada to thank lone voices and small groups of individuals who support each other in the face of systemic structural rigidity that tends to hinder experimentation and change. My best to Molly Evarts, Stephanie Froehle, Melanie Helle, April Honanie, Veronique Mertl, Taylor Cassidy, Stephanie Turcotte, Posie Kalin, Jason Miller, Dana Payne, Rama Devagupta, Mary Cushman, Jamie Ewing, Ai Addyson-Zhang, Kelly Thorson, Wendy Trummert, Necia

Kincaid, Ed Grode, Beth Trautman Atkerson, Tony Lyman, Katie Troia Stiles, Christine Collignon-Ray, Jeannine Medvedich, Nancy Spieker, and Noel Woods.

Teachers, parents, business leaders and concerned citizens, have also contributed to the growth of the processes and practices that are outlined in this book. A huge thank you to friends and companions who tirelessly contributed ideas, time, and business acumen over the past number of years. You will never know how much you sustained the forward progress. Best wishes to Kimberly Phillips, Paul Teske, Ed Bland, Michael Bledsoe, Liza Brown, Ashley Valentine, Chris Young, Anne TIpper, Maria Mackey Gunn, Paul O'Beirne, Rob Short, David French, Denis Adler, Raquel Carabine, Susanna Cunningham, Mona Kunselmann, Paul Fleming, Stephen Morrissey, Mike Pierson, Jay Lyman, and David Martin.

Many school districts have sprung into action, becoming early adopters in a field that as yet has not discovered its true potential. Foremost among them is Steilacoom Historical School District No. 1. It is indeed number one for a number of historical and methodological reasons. I am proud to work beside the superintendent, Kathi Weight and raft up with her amazing faculty and staff. Together, this community of teachers and learners is breaking new ground in areas of social emotional engagement, parent academy, mental health, academic performance and child well-being.

In the State of Washington, I am proud to be associated with future-facing leaders at organizations that are forging strong ties between learning communities, and methods that are based on emerging laboratory information with regard to memory processing and long-term potentiation. Thank you to Chris Reykdal, and educational leaders at the Washington Office of Superintendent of Public Instruction (OSPI) in Olympia, for your commitment to teachers across the State of Washington. I also want to acknowledge the Washington Association of Educators of the Talented and Gifted (WAETAG), a powerful voice for educators who strive to deliver first rate learning experiences for their young audiences. Thanks especially to Jen Flo, Robert Fawcett, and Amy Phillips who are tireless in their commitment to teachers and to the community which they serve.

Pockets of innovation exist where a dedication to an "early adopter" mentality highlights several champions in the field. Here, teachers are provisioned with co-created opportunities to rejuvenate learning spaces with high quality training that is carefully curated. Heartfelt appreciation to members of the leadership team and faculty at the Northwest Career and Technical Academy (NCTA) in Mt Vernon, WA. In particular, I want to thank Lynette Brower for her foresight and persistence in manifesting an ongoing professional development platform. In Hoquiam, WA, I have had the great privilege to work with Mary White and Laurie Gordon who invested so much energy and love into the design and implementation of their children's education. Co-creation of learning spaces is a universal solution to access, acceleration and affect. Affect delivers effect. I am so thankful for the cooperation and groundbreaking efforts at reform that are transforming schools across the State. Foremost among them is Challenger Middle and High School in the Bethel School District, Spanaway. I appreciate the leadership of Jeffrey Johnson and Kara Runge and delight in working with the high-school staff. It is exciting to also begin relationship-building and program development, with the new middle school staff.

In the Elma School District, I want to express my appreciation to Chris Nesmith and his amazing team of innovators, as he works ardently to ignite learning through an innovative mastery model that is engaging and meaningful for learners. Dr. Chris is supported by Neural Ed champion Wendy Beldin, who is advancing the program at every opportunity. I foresee great results from this whole school effort.

Thanks to my great friend Michael Peck for his vision, support and stepping in to help in areas in and outside the classroom. I am fortunate to have his insightful inquisition when we meet regarding the progress and continued vision of the movement. This Practical Guide too, was fortunate to receive a scholarship from the Charlotte Selva Estate which was awarded by the philanthropic efforts of another great friend - Jack Donnelly. Thank you to Jack and Charlotte.

I met Sandi Young through the courage and persistence of a 12-year-old boy in Tanzania, Uli, who against all odds is an accomplished and proud scholar, and well on his way to contribute great things to his community in high-school and beyond. The genius of technology and desire for learning is exemplified in his access to the outside world by means of a solar panel and an iPhone. The human brain is resilient and persistent. My gratitude to Sandi and to Uli.

Deep gratitude and many thanks to the book production team, especially to NoShooz Publishing, Inc. led by Caroline Doughty including Cameron and Keith Doughty, Libby Hawken, Kate Downes, Nathan Hall and Ovi.

Finally, this Practical Guide wouldn't be real without the acknowledgement of friends, colleagues and fellow reformers in educational spaces around the world. I am grateful for the friendship and collaborative work that is ongoing in Ireland with Patrick McAndrews, Katie Molony, Eva McMullan, and Kevin Burchaell. Grá agus míle buíochas díobh. It is gratifying to witness the inspiring work that my friend Rich Carr is accomplishing with workplace learning and talent development across the globe. A shout-out also to my friends in Bangalore, India. Thanks for your commitment to schools, Manjula Veerana, Shivaram K R, and Shyamala Kamath.

As ever, special thanks to JK and to JB. You are with me always.

Every learner learns differently, and is influenced by a complex combination of internal factors (biological, including neurobiological) and context (political, social, cultural, institutional, environmental, technological).

Therefore, receiving a personalized learning experience is an entitlement and a human right for every learner.

– UNESCO (Reimagining Education 2030)

Preface: Dear Reader...

Welcome to your cognitive revolution. I am so glad that you found your way to this Practical Guide. Each of us, whether we are parents or educators (or both), have been laboring in a cognitive world for a long time with tools that were designed for a behaviorist world. With the paradigm shift that accompanies this exploration, your life will experience many amazing changes. Expect greatness; enjoy the freedoms that will soon be self-evident; and especially, marvel at the impressive leaps your children and students will experience through implementation - leaps in autonomy, mastery, and purpose.

Why Every Educator Needs This Practical Guide

In retrospect, we confess that it often seems strange as we immerse our labors each day in neural development of young children with precariously scant, if any, knowledge about how the human brain works and how children learn. We might be the only profession that basically ignores the organ with which we are privileged to manipulate every day. It would equate to a heart surgeon offering to do a critical transplant when they had never studied the heart, or your car mechanic working on the engine of your new Tesla if they had never looked under the hood.

The solution for today's brain-based classroom didn't appear in any University Department or Learning laboratory or educational lecture hall. Instead, it spontaneously emerged from the school of nursing. Granted, I do have many degrees from the College of Education and have spent decades in schools and classrooms in many countries.

It also bears mentioning that neuroscience without learning sciences is simply brain science. There is nothing wrong with brain science but most brain scientists do not make great elementary or middle school teachers. And when we marry information about the human brain with a pedagogic model that is brain-aligned, learning spaces ignite.

The insights that are in this Practical Guide are not invented out of thin air. Nor are they solely theoretical. All strategies, hints, and suggestions come from hands-on trial-and-error experiences from teachers who have already walked this journey. They attended in-person, face-to-face institute coursework with hundreds of other teachers. Together, in an immersive learning space, they figured out how to implement a cognitive teaching and learning mode, often in spite of existing and deeply entrenched behaviorist school systems.

Each strategy, event, or plan had to be adjusted and massaged to fit their particular audience and environment. What worked for Ms. Pederson in an inner-city all-boys school in Detroit, didn't necessarily work for Miss Marion in her suburban community in South Dakota. However, there were aspects that could be shared from both settings that are appropriate for schools everywhere and for learning spaces that are very different from school. Teachers were not always successful and it was not always the same for all teachers – hence the broad spectrum of tools. But, the experiences were always meaningful and paved the way for outcomes that align as brain-based, social emotional, and academic in their unique circumstances.

One of our teachers put it succinctly and powerfully when she said, "Our results are always significant, and often breathtaking."

Our goal is twofold: (i) eliminate labeling and stratification in classrooms and, (ii) increase teacher capacity in this new educational field where neuroscience informs classroom practices and processes.

How to Use this Practical Guide

The Practical Guide has a simple layout mindful of accessibility and ease of use. We begin with a story – typically, a teacher wanted to implement a particular strategy so that a child or a situation could be made more successful.

The theme typically focuses on changing environments, rather than changing the child. The story gives way to a two-page spread in which the problem is described in a broad and general way on the left panel. First, we describe a behavior or a situation that is daily typical in a learning space. We then describe possible neural substrates that posit that situation. Opposite this on the right panel, we describe a solution. In each case, we look at the issues through a neural lens and focus the solution in a cognitive space. Each two-page spread is a separate and distinct unit that contains the problem and a solution that some educators have found useful in solving the situation.

Start Your Own Cognitive Revolution

All children have brains; all brains are unique. From that standpoint, it is not practicable to have a "one-size fits all" silver bullet strategy. Classroom activities and methods are therefore works in progress.

I like to view progress like a caterpillar emerging out of a cocoon. Ideas and strategies mature in a cocoon-like co-created incubator so that solutions emerge, alighting their delicate wings into our learning spaces like a butterfly set free.

With this Practical Guide, we invite you to co-create with us as you experiment - together we aspire to learn and nurture all children's brains through cognitive strategies. Teachers are key to helping all learners reach their full potential.

Best

Kieran O'Mahony, PhD, FRGS

Every Child has a Brain

Every brain has roughly 100 billion neurons

Every neuron has roughly 10,000 connections

Every child has trillions upon trillions of potential

Introduction: Ms. Pedersen's Story

Ms. Pedersen is an elementary teacher in a suburban area of a large American city. She has always been passionate about education and at times she says she loves her job. But she is also exhausted, exasperated, frustrated and disillusioned. "Burnout is real," she laughs with a shadow of sadness. She is a board-certified teacher, with aspirations to advance to graduate school. However, when she thinks about full-time work, raising her three children, and the prospect of a full-load in graduate school, she has come up to the line many times and balked.

Over the past two decades, she has been to countless trainings, innumerable team meetings, has withstood too many new principals and a few superintendents. Through it all, Ms. Pedersen has remained focused on the "kiddos" that she loves. Intuitively, she filters out what she knows will not work in her classroom, and she gravitates to practice with which she has had successes (no matter how limited) in the past.

Here is a view from the floor of her elementary world…

I have been in education for more than twenty years. I have seen a lot of change and I have modified my approach many times, sometimes voluntarily. Usually, the change happened when I had read an important new author or when a particular training was actually meaningful. However often, I changed because new and well-meaning administrators or principals expected it of me. Sadly, a lot of training sessions were not very appropriate for my students.

So, in my learning space – I try not to say classroom, although the children call it their classroom – there were tried and true methods that I invoked as critical. I used them every day for years. Some changes that I tried didn't last. In fact, they were eliminated rather immediately. Like the time that we were all told that children would focus better if we used large inflatable balls to sit on. That never worked for me and it caused a lot of chaos and contributed to children acting out. However, I kept one under inflated "ball-seat" for the kiddos, who on a day when they were stressed, would prefer to sit and feel the sensation of instability. There were class rules for behavior and this one was clear: as long as they don't interfere with the kiddos around them, they can sit on the bouncy ball seat.

I was careful to have a welcoming learning space. I stood at the door and welcomed the children into my space. Thinking back, we spent a lot of time trying to get the children to line up quietly and stand still. They had to remain in the hallway until they were lined up, quiet, and well-behaved (minus the squiggles). Today, I don't think that way. I open my arms and welcome them into the learning space where they feel safe and loved.

Our school had, and still has, policies about early morning activities. The plan was to be child-centric. When the child was dropped off, or the bus arrived, we were very mindful to be at the welcome point for them. We wanted them to be safe, welcome, and seen. We also liked to use the electronic notice board outside the main gate to wish happy birthday to the kiddos whose birthday coincided with the school day.

I had high expectations for the children when it came to managing themselves in the learning space. They are expected to know where to put their bags, their projects and any homework that requires turning in. Library books had to be returned in a timely manner. I had very strict repercussions for not getting these simple "entry tickets" right. If a child got all five days in the green, they were allowed Free Dress on Friday. On the other hand, if a child failed to get even one day correct, they would miss a recess, wouldn't get Free Dress Friday, and I had a serious chat with a parent.

Usually, all the children were able to get their body and materials under control by the second term. I found myself still having to use reminders for just a few stragglers. I used to feel so bad for these kiddos who seemed to fall further and further behind over the years. They simply could not keep up with the other students and I witnessed their life trajectories being so different.

It was a friend who teaches in a neighboring school district that first told me about Neural Ed and the Brain-Based Classroom. "The Best PD… EVER," was how Amy introduced me to it. The year before, I had heard a few rumblings through the grapevine, but I was always just too tired, too busy, or too overwhelmed. So it was with total surprise that I finished the first day of the Summer Institute with ease.

I wasn't in the slightest exhausted, overwhelmed, or flustered. I had assumed that neuroscience would be beyond my reach. They made it accessible and I wanted more. Simply referred to as the "Summer Institute," the two challenges on Day One of Neural Ed's training were mesmerizing. I learned that Neural Ed was short for The Institute for Connecting Neuroscience with Teaching and Learning. And it made sense. Of course I wanted to learn about the children's brains… hell, I wanted to know about my own brain. Who wouldn't?

I had been reluctant, mostly because of COVID, to attend an in-person immersive course for a full week (five days), but Amy assured me that I would not regret it. She came with me, attending her second in-service training as she had taken the course online the year before. "Face-to-face is always more fun," she laughed knowingly. So Monday morning found both of us grabbing a light breakfast with 150 other teachers at the Neural Ed PD location near Seattle, WA.

The surprise was immediate. How could I have missed this? We all missed it. Brand new vocabulary gave me access to incredible insights and new mental models that focused on how the human brain works and especially how children learn. I promptly eliminated several items from my bag of tricks – they were doing damage to the children. I resolved to get proficient in this new method with an eye on my ability to liberate children into their potential. I was excited to get started. Here are some of my highlights:

Plasticity:
I thought I knew about plasticity, but *nothing* I was doing in my learning space was contributing to the child's ability to take advantage of this neural ability. It didn't even enter onto my radar! Today, I am very purposeful about saying the words neural plasticity (and not just plasticity). I began teaching the meaning of malleability to the kiddos. I tell them that the brain is like jello – whatever shape we use to wait for liquid jello to set (the container) will dictate the end product. If I pour a hot mix into a bowl it will look like a bowl, if I put it into a mouse-shaped container – it will end up looking like a mouse. Kids get that.

Potential:
I quickly realized I didn't have an accurate notion of a child's potential. Imagine my surprise to find out that every child in my learning space had as many neurons as myself – one hundred billion. And that each neuron establishes roughly 10,000 connections at the synapse. That equates to trillions upon trillions of potential connections. By comparison, my smart phone only uses 2 billion transactions. Yet, it can accomplish amazing feats of speech recognition and translation to any language in the world – which leads me to believe that every child has exponential capacity beyond the smartphone. Yet, I was not able to unleash that kind of power for my kiddos. Today I can.

Synapse:
This term was also new to me. I had heard of it, but had no idea what it was for and how important it was in the learning process. Today I know that synapse is the "currency of learning." Things that I can do, words that I say, practices that I am intentional about... all these help the child learn at the synapse.

Just this shift in my thinking, with these new vocabulary words helped me reinvent my teaching career. Some changes were tiny, but had a huge effect – like intentional eyeball-to-eyeball contact with my students. And, I am always aware that there might be a child who is sad, struggling, and alone. Here are some of the other things I did immediately that had a forever impact on my work.

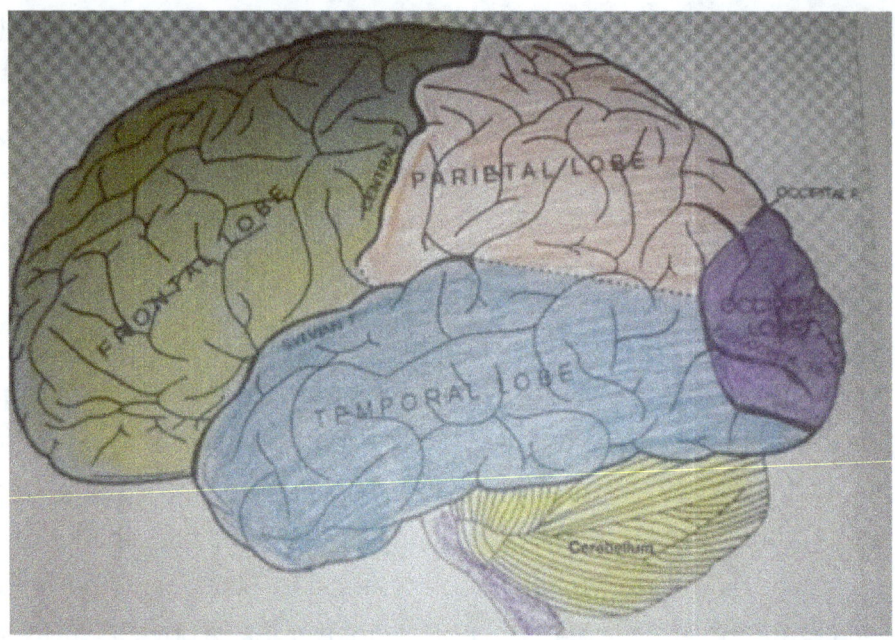

Figure 1. Cerebellum and Four Lobes: Occipital, Temporal, Parietal and Frontal

I abandoned all punishments. I gave up all rewards. No more stars, no more token economies. And especially, I stopped public shaming. Those easy-to-use Point Systems on Smart Boards that I assumed were making my life more efficient were actually destroying motivation and causing students to act up. They were taking refuge in oppositional behavior, and thus caused me to react with punitive threats and strict disciplinary outcomes. It was a sad, engrossing and negative spiral that I initiated unwittingly by my lack of understanding of the Reticular Activating System, the Amygdala Hijack and the Involuntary Reactive Impulsivity associated with boredom and anxiety.

So now, I begin each day with a "soft start." Children take care of their needs without stress or prodding. We always spend a few minutes bouncing balls so that their working memory is cleared out and they are ready for learning.

And the most important outcome of this neural lens has been an unexpected benefit: I have less stress in *my* life and a whole lot more time to do the things that I like to do. For instance, this Spring, I signed up for graduate work through an online university that allows me to pursue my interest in the neuroscience of learning. I will use data from the learning space that has evolved with me on this amazing journey into the brain.

I learned a very important lesson that began my journey. There is a difference between managing a class and managing a brain.

I had been trained to manage classrooms, but I had no idea about the brain. For me, I was a stranger in a strange land. It was scary at times!

And I learned that I was really good at it. Who would have known? Making a few simple changes in vocabulary could cause such a cascade of mindset and mental model application in everything we do.

At times, concepts like amygdala, hippocampus, and cerebellum seemed strange — that was until I learned that these terms are simply Latin words that describe the shapes of key brain structures. I now enjoy learning and talking about the brain "almond," brain "Sea Horse," and "Little Brain."

I developed a strong intuitive instinct about how to engage children and I was good at sensing when something was not quite to the mark. What I didn't anticipate and what turned out to be true genius was this – when I learned the science behind why something didn't work, it changed everything. For the first time it made sense.

And then I realized that this work with my brain percolated into every single thing I did every single day. Every thought, every word, every idea all made sense when rooted in the brain. In retrospect, that of course makes sense, because we are who we are because of our brains.

Electrocorticography is useful in the hospital and delivers best results.

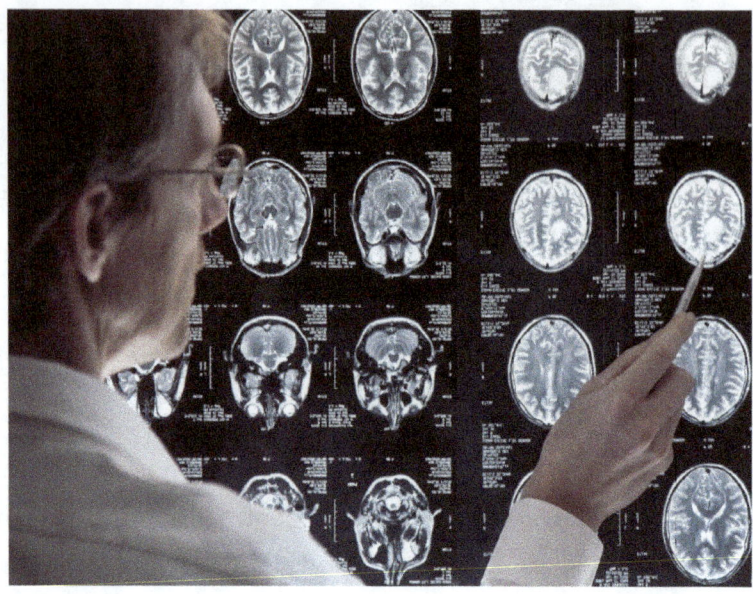

How to interpret a child's behavior is useful in the learning space and delivers best results.

Section I: Regulate

When a child is dysregulated, escalated, or in an amygdala hijack, this is not the time to reason. This is a time for co-regulation.

– Kieran O'Mahony, PhD, FRGS

Today's children are essentially hunter gatherers... They have inbuilt instincts that were designed to work best in tall grass at a time when cats were big.

— Kieran O'Mahony, PhD, FRGS

Our House

It can happen in all homes. Children have the same mom, same dad, same food, same schools, same churches, same restaurants – everything's the same for each child. But let's take a look at one family in particular with a young boy, Raphael, and a girl, Serena. If we visit their living room on any average Tuesday, we'll find them finishing up homework, texting their friends, and watching TV late into the evening.

Suddenly, mom realizes that it is bedtime. "Serena," she interrupts her daughter's Instagram messages with her friend Yvonne. "You have swim program in the morning. Have you even started preparing your lunch yet? Stop texting your friends, put that phone away and get ready for school in the morning."

Serena rolls her eyes, finishes up one last text, throws her phone into her school bag, and moves into the kitchen to make the dreaded lunch. "Mom overreacts," she thinks to herself, but says nothing to stir the pot. "What about him?" She casts a cold eye at Raphael, her parting shot as she leaves the room.

Mom is ready. She immediately turns her attention to Raphael. He, too, was engrossed online with his buddies. He had a headset on and was smiling happily at something that mom can't hear. She waved her hands to break into his attention, peeved at how slow he is at removing the headset to glance in her direction. "Hello!" she yells over the headset, "I'm talking to you. It's late. Stop texting Peter, put that computer and phone away, and get your soccer gear ready for the morning."

"It's not Peter," Raphael is visibly upset that she accused him wrongly. "I'm finishing my science with Vincent."

"Well put that phone away and go to bed." She grabbed the moment to make an adjustment to the soccer craze. "Last week, you destroyed my bathroom with your muddy boots. Tomorrow, clean the boots on the field before you leave. Don't bring them into my bathroom. Now finish up and go to sleep. I won't be able to get you out of bed in the morning as usual."

Raphael didn't look at his mother while he was closing his computer, putting his phone in his pocket, and collecting his science homework. He stalked out of the living room and closed the door in his own room firmly. "Mom hates me," he felt that familiar voice reminding him. "Serena is no help, she hates me too. I hate school. I don't even like soccer. I can't sleep. I don't want to go to bed. I can't finish my science."

He could hear his mom complaining about him to his dad down in the living room, even over the sound of the news channel. "That child will be the death of me. What in God's name is the matter with him? He'll never amount to anything."

Dad muttered something that sounded like agreement. "Just like your crazy brother." Or, it could have been "lazy brother." It was hard to make out.

"Dad hates me too." His head was spinning and he was sad.

After a long time, Raphael finally quieted down sufficiently to get a few hours of sleep. In the morning, he was in a deep dark dream where he was falling off a cliff – when his mother broke in and threatened to pull him out on the floor if he didn't look lively.

"I don't wanna go to school, I feel sick." His pleading tone was completely ignored by mom who was already scrambling to get to work herself.

"Get out of bed this instant. I don't have time to play games with you. Your sister was up and went out to swim with your daddy a whole hour ago! What is wrong with you? You'll make me late again." She was throwing his clothes on the blanket on top of him. Her voice was penetrating. "Get dressed and get into the car. You can eat a slice of toast on the way."

Later that day, he told the coach that he was giving up soccer. Coach reminded him that he had to play *some* team sport and suggested lacrosse in the spring.

Imagine how different life would be in Raphael and Serena's household if Mom and Dad had some neural adjustment in their mental models about how children's brains worked and how that affected their minds, their beliefs, their mental wellbeing and their physical health?

Instead of setting Raphael upon a path where it was not only easy to give up on soccer or science or life, it was required for his own safety and sanity. How could it be that Serena and Raphael are so vastly different, even though they came from exactly the same place, household, and parents?

It may seem strange, but this is exactly how it is supposed to happen. Each individual brain is unique, wired for personalized growth and individual identity. From a neuroscientific perspective, each brain is differentially hardwired and susceptible to social context. From a parental and teaching perspective this is ideal, because parents and teachers have control over social context and can address and influence the hardwired and plastic parts as needed.

If Mom, realizing that their son, Raphael, was wired ultra-sensitive because of genetic components that both she and his biological dad were instrumental in providing, she would have chosen to adjust the environment, rather than trying to adjust him. She would have started by taking a deep breath and using different words and body language. It might have gone like this…

"Raphael, it's time for bed. You have soccer tomorrow… Do you need help finishing your homework or getting your gear ready?"

This acknowledgment of his sensitivity to language and social setting would not have catapulted him into a negative spiral that had the power to change his life journey and his identity. Just knowing that one of their children was highly resilient (Serena) and the other highly sensitive (Raphael), would inform Mom and Dad about how to co-create a safe psychological environment where both their children could thrive.

This is but the tip of the iceberg. Recognizing our own and our children's neurobiological hardwiredness to social context, is a critical step in being predictable, consistent, and kind.

In this Practical Guide, you will find ideas and strategies to inform the way you approach education – in particular with mental models and mindset, that enhance learning and offer a healthy and meaningful life trajectory.

Growing a brain is a neural exercise based on new evolutionary structures that must inhibit long-standing primitive defensive systems.

– Kieran O'Mahony, PhD FRGS

School Sucks!

School sucks!
Teachers suck!
Everything about learning sucks!

Like much of what happens in school, the "suck syndrome" is highly contagious.

There is always one child (or a clique) that dominates the negative. No matter how hard the teacher tries; no matter how interesting the lesson is, that child will complain and have a bad attitude.

The child shows up in school with an inherited attitude. They have already learned from previous experience that "school sucks"... and teachers suck.

What's Really Happening?

Many things can contribute to a negative mindset. And as a teacher, you will probably not have control over most of them – they can happen with peers, in the home, the community, as well as previous school experiences. But there are many things teachers can do to contribute to a shift in mindset:

One, understand what "mindset" really is. When we understand mindset, we can help the student also understand its deep meaning and truly gain **AGENCY** over their own mindset.

Two, use concrete strategies to teach the power of mindset. Strategies help children see mindset as changeable, a *continuum*. In other words, we are not "stuck" in a particular mindset – we can ALL change our understanding and our place on the continuum any time.

What would you rather be, growth or fixed mindset? Most people will say they are Growth Mindset. However, it is not that simple. For an individual teacher it might look a lot like *retro-active inhibition*. In other words, children who think that everything about school "sucks" have already learned this somewhere else at an earlier time and are showing up with their negative mindset – unprepared for learning.

The Mindset Continuum: Intelligence

Some children have already experienced sad and negative things that convince them that life in school is all bad. What can a teacher do? Begin with *mindset*. Show the children that intelligence and mindset are plastic by building a physical Continuum along a wall.

Mindset Continuum

Benefits

- Children think about their own intelligence.
- They see intelligence as a continuum between Fixed and Growth.
- As children physically move along the continuum, they psychologically shift their thinking from Fixed to Growth.
- Makes a child's thinking visible to themselves.
- Makes a child's thinking visible to the teacher.
- Making ideas visible is a concrete step to understanding ideas like plasticity.

How to Do it

1. Use Flip Chart sheets to draw a **Continuum Line** at shoulder height on a back wall.
2. On one end write the word **GROWTH**; on the other end write **FIXED**. Starting at the Growth end, write these words along the line in equal sections towards the Fixed end:
   Agree a lot – Agree a little – Don't know – Disagree a little – Disagree a lot
3. Ask children to place themselves on the line based on their response to a *Likert Scale* question such as "How much do you agree with this statement? *You are born with a certain amount of intelligence, and that's all you get!*"

💡 Try this exercise in the Faculty room too! This makes visible what teachers know about mindset.

I'm No Good at...

"Math! Reading! Basketball...!"

This is a very common statement and very real belief among children in school. But the truth is, many adults also think this way. How many people do you know who say, "I couldn't do that..." or "No way, that's impossible!"

Just like intelligence, people also have beliefs about how talent works. And just like intelligence, talent is malleable.

What's Really Happening?

Think of fish in a tank. Imagine that you put a glass wall to divide the tank in two. The fish can only swim to the wall and remain in the small area that is cordoned off by the glass sides. After some time, remove the glass wall. The fish continues to swim only to the center remembering the limitations that were placed by the previous geography. We habituate to what seems real.

In Skinner's *Walden Two,* he describes an enclosure for his sheep that defines a grazing zone without fences. Surprisingly, the sheep are bounded by a circle of string. When the farmer wants to move the sheep to a fresh grazing zone, he simply moves the string. Upon investigation, we discover that the farmer started out with an electric fence by which the sheep learned to avoid a nasty shock. When the fence was replaced with a string, the sheep continued to be guided by the associated nasty memory.

This is a simple example of **Associationism** resulting in **Active Avoidance**. The fish and sheep associated boundaries with a previous experience and were careful to actively avoid them. The same thing happens with children who have a bad experience at school, such as scoring low on a math test or not making the basketball team. In order to not feel that disappointment again, they might practice active avoidance.

The Mindset Continuum: Talent

When we understand neural plasticity, we can accept the limitless potential of all our children. As in the intelligence continuum, show the children that *talent* and mindset are plastic by building a physical Continuum along a wall. Based on the children's response, place them on the continuum between Fixed and Growth to make visible their talent mindset.

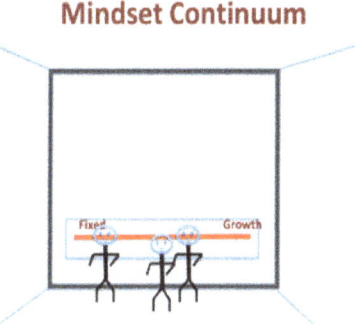

Benefits

- Children think about their own ability.
- They realize talent is a result of effort.
- Begin to understand that they are in control and can decide to be anywhere on the continuum.
- Makes a child's thinking visible to themselves.
- Makes a child's thinking visible to the teacher.
- Making ideas visible is a concrete step to understanding ideas like plasticity.

How to Do it

1. Use Flip Chart sheets to draw a **Continuum Line** at shoulder height on a back wall.

2. On one end write the word **GROWTH**; on the other end write FIXED. Starting at the Growth end, write these words along the line in equal sections towards the Fixed end: **Agree a lot – Agree a little – Don't know – Disagree a little – Disagree a lot**

3. Ask children to place themselves on the line based on their response to a Likert Scale question such as "How much do you agree with this statement? You are born with a certain amount of talent, and that's all you get!"

💡 Talent is a derivative of *effort* – it can be improved with cognitive rehearsal and myelin.

Avoid Challenges

In theory, it is a good idea to present children with challenges so that they can "stretch" themselves intellectually and make a valid attempt to solve the challenge.

In practice, it quickly becomes apparent that some children excel and even welcome difficult challenges, while other children abhor challenges and avoid them.

Every time a child fails to solve a challenge, they want to avoid it even more. They confirm to themselves that they are "no good" at this kind of learning. So, they follow simple instructions and do the least amount to get by under the radar. But as their teacher, you know that this child has way more to offer. It may also seem that the child is afraid to look like the odd man out, to be labeled as not good enough or even look stupid in front of classmates, so they avoid new challenges.

What's Really Happening?

Rather than learn and grow, the child is more driven by the desire to look smart. The child will not necessarily know this, nor be able to articulate this notion if asked. However, to you it may be more than obvious.

The mindset surrounding that desire to look smart, translates into motivation driven by an involuntary need for **self-preservation**. The sensitive child views a challenge as something that will make them look dumb in front of peers.

The survival instincts of the hindbrain kick in. It is a safer choice to avoid the challenge, than risk rejection by looking like a failure in front of friends and teachers.

We can change the desire to avoid challenges and preserve the self, by helping a child understand the difference between Fixed and Growth mindset.

The Mindset Continuum: Challenges

This exercise gives children the ability to create their own tool to gauge their mindset about avoiding or embracing challenges. We create a sliding scale with an avoidant RED Zone (Fixed mindset) and an embracing GREEN Zone (Growth mindset).

Benefits

- The child will learn new vocabulary to discuss their feelings and experiences.
- The child will see themselves on a continuum of growth, rather than a fixed state of ability.
- The child will associate the physical ability to shift on the continuum with their mental shift.
- Children enjoy building the concrete scaffold, giving them a sense of purpose and immediate mastery.

How to Do it

1. Cut strips of red-green gradient paper for each student. Or, tape equal parts red, yellow, and green paper together to make your own gradient. Laminate the strip with thick lamination for strength and durability.

2. Help the child punch a hole on each side margin of the strip. Insert a pipe cleaner through one end. Help the child feed one bead onto the pipe cleaner as shown, then feed the open end of the pipe cleaner through the other end to secure it.

3. The child can now move the bead from the RED Zone to the GREEN Zone, demonstrating how our approach to challenges can change.

💡 It is important to co-create the model with the student so they can achieve agency.

Give up Easily

Obstacles crop up for learners when they are trying to finish a project or turn in an assignment on time.

Some children seem to be able to put their heads down and persist in the face of setbacks. These same children show their resilience and bounce back with seemingly little effort even with obstacles in other places – such as on the soccer field or playground.

But, other children will come face-to-face with an obstacle and give up easily. Overwhelmed and helpless, no amount of assistance will get these children to a place of self-efficacy and success. Over time, the child tends to fall further and further behind.

These situations are a common source of frustration for both the student and the teacher.

What's Really Happening?

Children do not know when they are stuck in a fixed mindset. Many children have difficulty projecting their image into an abstract notion like mindset. But understanding this theory of mind, is a crucial developmental pillar that allows the learner to make strides along the mindset continuum between fixed and growth.

Similarly, children can be unaware of the unhelpful consequences of persistent negative self-talk. It won't be obvious to them that negativity feeds their reticular activating system by reinforcing a downward spiral of ineffective processing. A mind stuck in negative self-talk becomes a self-fulfilling prophecy, so that the child accepts the notion of giving up easily. This does no favors for the child's advancement in school.

Learned "helplessness" is a phenomenon that infiltrates learning systems when mental models that personify negativity are allowed to take root and proliferate. It cannot be "talked down" because the child will not have access to a rational brain to entertain the logic involved in defusing it. We must take a different approach.

The Mindset Continuum: Persistence

This exercise helps a child see how their ability to persist is not fixed – even when a number of mental and genetic factors may be causing the child to feel in a stuck place. The child can learn a great deal about resilience and a capacity for bouncing back with the aid of these tactile charts.

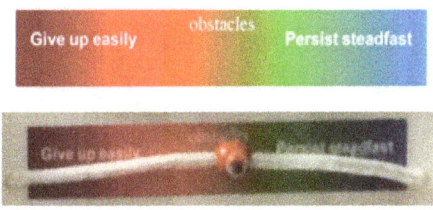

Benefits

- Children gain a simple mental model to help them bounce back from negative self-talk.
- They learn new vocabulary to discuss their approach to obstacles.
- The child will see themselves on a continuum of growth, rather than a fixed state.
- Children enjoy building the concrete scaffold, giving them a sense of purpose and immediate mastery.

How to Do it

1. Cut strips of red-green gradient paper for each student. Or, tape equal parts red, yellow, and green paper together to make your own gradient. Laminate the strip with thick lamination for strength and durability.

2. Help the child punch a hole on each side margin of the strip. Insert a pipe cleaner through one end. Help the child feed one bead onto the pipe cleaner as shown, then feed the open end of the pipe cleaner through the other end to secure it.

3. The child can now move the bead from the RED Zone to the GREEN Zone as needed, demonstrating how an approach to challenges can change from "giving up easily" to "persisting through" obstacles.

💡 The hands-on tactile scaffold helps myelinate a new mental model towards growth.

Effort is Fruitless

Picture this: A teacher spends time and is careful and thoughtful about new material. A child appears to take in the information and apply it in practice. The child completes several more practices as homework.

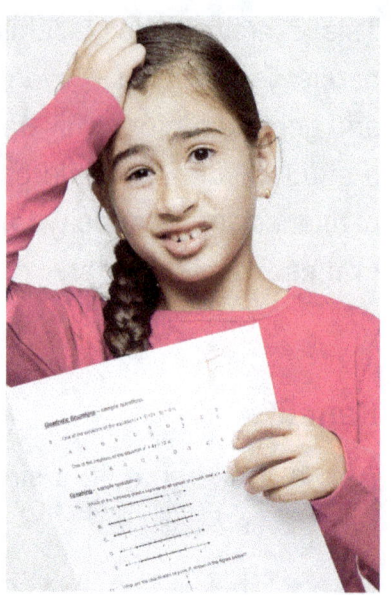

The child turns in the assignment and the teacher grades it. Sadly, the child showed that the understanding which had appeared earlier in the day did not stick – they got most of the assignment wrong. There were a lot of red marks and they received a C- grade.

From the teacher's point of view, this is clearly an opportunity to roll up the sleeves, review the material, and uncover where the misunderstanding lies. From the child's viewpoint, all those red marks are clear evidence that the effort they put into the work didn't pay off. The effort was wasted. They are convinced that it is time to give up.

What's Really Happening?

It is very common for miscommunication to hijack a thoughtful teacher's efforts. While the teacher is under the impression that the child will benefit from a focus on the corrections, the student has already passed the point of no return. The effort was difficult; it was a painful reminder that they were not capable; that their intelligence failed them once again. It was time to give up on effort.

The brain filter (the Reticular Activating System) has confirmed a deep-seated belief: "I am no good at this work and there is no point putting any effort into it." No matter what the teacher practices with regard to trying to make the student see that the corrections are easy and that the solution is perseverance, the student is not able to process that knowledge. Their brain is negating the teacher's efforts.

The Mindset Continuum: Effort

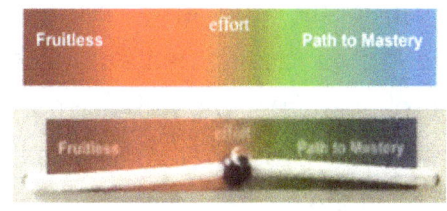

The hands-on scaffold is a simple, colorful, and tactile way to meet the child where they are struggling and help them get out of a stuck mentality about processing information. The first thing this teaches is that there is a choice. Choice connects to autonomy and sets them on the path to intrinsic motivation. After choice comes mastery. They are able to make the scaffold model, and move from Red towards Green, as far as they choose. Finally, they will achieve their purpose: to place themselves in a position for improved success through effort.

Benefits

- The child will have fun building the scaffold.
- They will envision a physical shift along a continuum.
- They will be able to substitute themselves for the bead and googly eye and see they have the power to master anything through effort.

How to Do it

1. Create a similar scaffold as in the Mindset Continuum Challenge, but with **Effort** as the construct, RED Zone as "Fruitless" and GREEN Zone as "Path to Mastery."

2. Invite the child to add more meaningful words so that they can access the construct. Fruitless might be more meaningful as "No Good" or "Hard."

3. Work with the child as they laminate, drill and install the bead and pipe cleaner so that they can visualize and articulate the continuum from Fixed (Red) to Growth (Green).

💡 Help the child demonstrate the finished scaffold to another child who is also stressed.

Ignore Useful Negative Criticism

Even today, I can remember my math teacher returning our corrected assignments and seeing Teacher's bold red strokes. It's a painful memory. Criticism shows us our mistakes, cruelly reminding us that Mary always gets an A+, while I am lucky to get a C-.

No one told us to compare our scores with the other kids, or to focus only on the wrong answers. It seemed like we were always moving interminably forward at a speed that prevented us from keeping up.

Eventually, to avoid the painful feeling of criticism, children will ignore assignment scores and stop caring if they get A's or C's. They ignore useful feedback, not realizing how helpful criticism like that can be. This negative thinking will follow them for life.

What's Really Happening?

Labeling and stratifying children are byproducts of assessment methods that render grades on a one-size-fits-all "bell curve" process. Children who are able will appear to do well in this system, while learners who are not able, will fall further and further behind – in spite of all kinds of support mechanisms and measures designed specifically to decrease learning lags and increase academic performance.

The truth is, these same children who seem to not be able to compete well in class are capable and willing to try in other areas in and outside school. It might not appear to make sense that a child would excel at math but find reading difficult, or thrive on the soccer pitch but struggle to write essays or articulate ideas.

It all comes down to autonomic nervous system reactivity – a child's tendency towards sensitivity versus resilience. Neurobiologically, some people are more resilient than others. They can bounce back quicker and without proactive negative consequences that tend to hinder their progress. Yet, all children can learn to accept feedback and grow from it.

The Mindset Continuum: Criticism

For highly sensitive children, criticism is always negative. No matter how it is packaged, no matter how careful we are, it seems that criticism has the exact opposite effect on their attitude and their ability.

Mindset is both a doorway into resolving this crisis, as well as a foundational pillar that causes it. When the child is convinced that intelligence and talent are fixed – that is, born with what I have and can't really do anything to change it – then this tangible exercise brings physical proof to the table.

- The child begins to explore criticism as something other than negative feedback.
- The child can place themselves on a continuum that is not permanent.
- The child makes progress with mental models that are rooted in growth mindset thinking.

How to Do it

1. Create a similar scaffold as in the Mindset Continuum Challenge, but with Criticism as the topic, RED Zone as "Ignore Negative" and GREEN Zone as "Learn From."

2. Help the child use meaningful vocabulary for the developmental stage they are at. **Criticism** can have a negative connotation; make it fun and welcoming for them.

3. Demonstrate with the child how easy it is to learn from fun mistakes and how easy it is to move oneself from the RED Zone to the GREEN one.

💡 The more a child discusses their feelings and articulates experiences, the more white matter strengthens their growth mindset.

Threatened by Success of Others

Roughly 25% of children in your care can be triggered by their social context. It might be the classroom, the cafeteria, the playground, the ride to school, or the incident in the hallway before class.

What it means for you, is that the child who is hypersensitive will be less able to engage in social activities like learning. Even more, your body language, words, and actions could contribute to their thinking that confirms the belief that they are not good enough or not as bright as other kids.

When other children are enthusiastic about showing their work or their amazing ability to solve problems, this child might feel threatened by others' obvious successes. They respond by disengaging or acting out.

What's Really Happening?

Sensory information from visual, auditory, tactile, taste and smell bring information into the brain. The information is invariably routed through the seat of emotional processing, the amygdala. Depending on the metabolic state of the amygdala, or how hyperactive it is, the information is then sent to either the rational thinking brain or to the reactive involuntary brain.

As teachers, we would hope that a child's amygdala sends information to the executive higher-order site of processing. But more often than not, it is sent to the hindbrain reactive place. A persistent "amygdala hijack" causes them to lose access to their rational "higher-order thinking" brain for learning.

Here, the only option for the child is a freeze, fight, flight, or fawn response. Any of these choices are not conducive to learning – at least the kind of learning that you as a teacher are anticipating. In order to facilitate the child's attention to positive thinking and enjoyment in school, it is necessary to adjust their thinking system to embrace a growth mindset.

The Mindset Continuum: Success of Others

When you get your eyesight tested at the optometrist, they don't give you a range of ten or fifteen choices. They simply ask, is it better or worse?

It works the same for the sensitive child. Would you like to be threatened by or inspired by the success of others? Binary concrete tangibles align with Miller's Law, so that the child's working memory is protected from cognitive overload and a heavy sense of overwhelm.

- The child can choose easily between two options.
- The child learns to articulate feelings and aspirations.
- It is a fast and fulfilling way to experience mental shifts and feel the difference immediately.

How to Do it

1. Create a similar scaffold as in the Mindset Continuum Challenge, but with **Success of Others** as the topic, RED Zone as "Threatened By" and GREEN Zone as "Inspired By." Play with the notion of Better or Worse at the Optometrist's office.

2. Ask the child how they would like to feel when they see another child succeeding, and invite them to move their bead along the continuum. The difference between being threatened or inspired by the success of your peers can be expressed as simply as a quick shift along a short continuum.

3. Invite the child to share how it feels when someone else is inspired by their recent success at school, in sports, or other hobbies.

💡 About 25% of your students will be less resilient than others in social settings.

Plateau Early, Fail to Reach Potential

For the learner who appears stuck in the Red Zone of the mindset charts, difficulties and consequences will impact their journey through school and, indeed, in life.

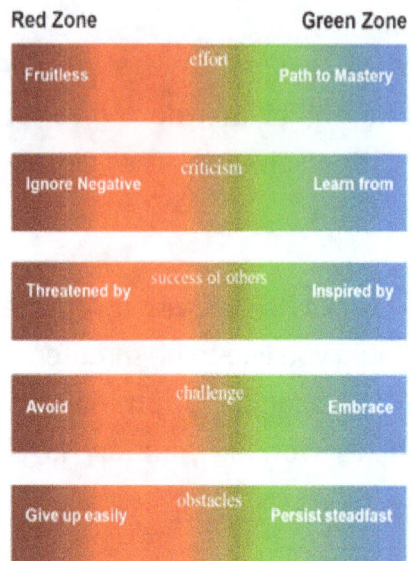

Think about any child that avoids challenges, gives up easily, sees effort as fruitless, ignores useful criticism, and feels threatened by the success of others. Each negative mindset wields a heavy multiplicative effect on the next.

It is for this reason that the child tends to plateau early in academic achievement and, even though mom or dad thinks their child has much more potential, all indicators point to a different outcome. The teacher, also, might be frustrated by the child's lack of forward motion and has already exhausted all supplementary interventions that the system offers.

What's Really Happening?

When children fail to attain their true potential, what it really means is that the adult doesn't know how to access their neural plasticity. Teachers must understand neural plasticity - every child has access to trillions upon trillions of white matter structures that enhance their learning capacity. These structures have names, and educators know how to myelinate these structures.

When parents and teachers do not own a foundational knowledge of neuroscience and related pedagogic models, the students are at the mercy of mindset definitions that are ill-informed.

And knowledge alone is not enough. Methods must be grounded in practice that is informed by neural approaches. We begin with vocabulary that abandons behavior and embraces cognition. We build structures with an informed mindset. We deliver with passion. Success happens when adults follow a child's appetite, knowing that aptitude follows.

The Complete Mindset Continuum

To paraphrase the psychologist Piaget, children need scaffolds that are concrete when they have not yet accessed their higher-order cognitive functions for theory of mind and further abstract thinking.

In the mindset exercises, we move at a slow pace with one construct at a time. We focused on these five constructs: Challenges, Obstacles, Effort, Criticism, and Success of Others. Now, let's bring them together to help children develop a deeper understanding of how mindset works – and varies person-to-person – on a larger scale.

- Children can get a concrete idea of where their mindset falls in different areas and across the board.
- They recognize that everyone has a slightly different mindset.
- Builds tolerance for ambiguity and reduces cognitive load to free up working memory.

How to Do it

1. Gather all your Mindset Continuum models and co-create a one-page spread with your students.

2. Provide the opportunity to play with the different zones by moving beads back and forth.

3. Invite children to teach peers who have not yet been introduced to Mindset.

💡 Examining Mindset through concrete exercises helps children reach their potential.

Deterministic Worldview

Mindset is important in school and it is increasingly more important in the journey through life. A fixed mindset can deter a child from thriving in a learning environment, because it blocks them from accessing all the neural capacity of their being. They end up settling for outcomes that do not reflect their true potential.

Furthermore, fixedness leads to a worldview that also limits a person's aspirations and dreams. When a child believes that all things in life are pre-determined, they develop learned helplessness. Such a deterministic worldview defines and often limits a person's attention, intention, and comprehension.

The idea of malleability on the other hand, as defined by a growth mindset, allows children to take charge of their learning and be more intentional in their life journey. Agency in these arenas offers a greater sense of personal freedom.

What's Really Happening?

When one believes that intelligence, talent, and other qualities are innate and unchangeable, then there are limits to learning, understanding, and engagement with life itself. It is important that we as parents and teachers not only understand the implications of mindset, but are also proficient with teaching techniques that liberate all learners into their potential.

The importance of vocabulary cannot be overstated. When a child is able to articulate a shift on a continuum between Fixed to Growth with the help of these exercises, that child is beginning to set new neuron tracts in place and strengthen them with myelin, so that real change can occur in the learning space, as well in the life choices.

Words are key to articulation, thinking is key to manifestation, and change is the outcome.

Greater Sense of Personal Freedom

When faced with something novel and somewhat different, many people will immediately say, "I can't do that!" And in fact, they often prove that they cannot do it.

However, when we change our words to something like this, "Ooh, that looks interesting, I am going to try to do that," a very different outcome can unfold. In a simple exercise, invite children to connect positive language to events or lessons where they achieve mastery.

Benefits

- The child will experience a greater sense of personal freedom.
- The child will see that negative thinking actually is real.
- The child will consolidate a deep and enduring understanding of the power of mindset.

How to Do it

1. Demonstrate that a positive affirmation like "I can do this" can lead to more positive outcomes in any subject area.

2. Create space for the child to gain confidence by aligning positive self-talk with moments of mastery and visible success.

3. Resist the temptation to reward the positive outcomes. If you must say anything about the success, praise the *effort*, not the child.

💡 Brain is not destiny. Billions of neurons give us limitless potential to grow, adapt, change.

Asking Questions Won't Work

When we think of a traditional school, we often envision a teacher standing in front of the children who are enthusiastically clamoring to shout out the right answer to a question posed to the class.

Yet, teachers who are in the field long enough will confirm that such question and answer methodologies are rarely successful. For every enthusiastic hand-waving child, there are many more students who fall by the wayside. These children, who never volunteer an answer and who are intimidated by the manner of learning where they feel put on the spot, feel publicly exposed for their lack of knowledge.

This kind of public shaming is not intentional by the teacher.
In fact, teachers join the profession to accomplish the exact opposite, and are most fulfilled when they see lightbulbs going off for even the most frightened struggling learner.

So why do teachers persist in this kind of direct question technique day after day, as if we are living in a Ferris Bueller movie? Anyone, anyone?

What's Really Happening?

Life would be so much easier in the classroom if all children would be willing and able to keep up with the pace. Some kids can answer questions... but others don't seem to be able to.

Typically, about 50% of students are on track. Another 15% are often at risk. They seem to be sporadic at paying attention, but are always on the cusp of distraction. The rest of the children, when they show up at all, are downright difficult to teach. These are the high-risk learners. They seem ill-prepared for the grade they are in and struggle to keep up each day. The worst part is, they tend to lag farther and farther behind over weeks and months and eventually settle for a grade way below what should be their potential. They rarely do well with this type of questioning.

Predictable, Consistent & Kind

Asking direct questions might be predictable, but there is no consistency in whether a child might be publicly shamed for lack of the right answer. And having to answer questions in front of the class might feel very unkind to some kids. In fact, for many children the art of questioning is predictably and consistently unkind.

A very simple formula allows all children to learn: make school predictable, consistent and kind. Using this method ensures all children have a structure that opens the mind for learning.

Benefits

- Predictability frees up much needed working memory so the brain can focus on new material.
- Consistency grows the Uncinate Fasciculus allowing the child to interpret past memories in order to make decisions for the present or future.
- Kindness moderates the amygdala's metabolic state so that it sends new information to the prefrontal cortex.

How to Do it

1. Invite the child to reflect **alone** on new material using a carefully curated three-question scaffold that connects the survival, emotional, and rational brain.

2. Ask these three questions: What was surprising? What did you know already, but now see differently? What do you still need help with?

3. Invite children to **revise their thinking** by sharing their reflection with peers in a safe group setting.

💡 An iterative teaching model that is predictable, consistent and kind, works every time.

Scaffolds can be Ineffective

Scaffolds are temporary structures that support people while working on buildings. In education, scaffolds are physical or conceptual aids (like rubrics) that support the student in learning a new skill or idea.

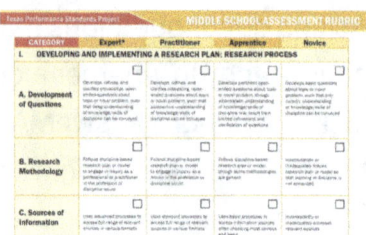

In theory, a scaffold is the right way to go. Any tool that helps children develop their minds and gain a deeper understanding should work, right?

Unfortunately, scaffolds often backfire, leaving the student floundering and the teacher frustrated. A scaffold that works for some children may not be useful for all children. So how could we choose a simple scaffold that allows all children to flourish?

Rubrics are very useful tools for teachers that lay out a path for excellence – they are a roadmap for a good grade. So why do children ignore rubrics and fail to score as well as they could?

What's Really Happening?

Rubrics almost always break Miller's Law. It is easy to rectify. Miller's Law states that our span of immediate memory or judgment is limited to about 7 (+/- 2) pieces of information. More modern research shows that the number is likely closer to 3 (+/- 2). Teachers typically work at the low end of the law - one new concept at a time.

In essence, a child has a very limited capacity to absorb new pieces of information at a time. A comprehensive or expansive rubric overwhelms most children with too much information, and they tune out. When we give too many choices, or too many sentences to comprehend, we defeat the purpose of a rubric.

Scaffolds can be Amazing

Since we Teach to the Orchid, we use the lower end of Miller's Law (3 pieces of information) when making scaffolds like rubrics. With less information to take in, children get the benefits of predictable, consistent, and kind teaching methods. As one student put it, "We always know what is happening, what's coming next and we never get lost."

When you are doing this correctly, the children are doing all the work and the teacher becomes more like a facilitator.

Benefits

- Children feel more agency over their school work when they are not overwhelmed with too many ideas or expectations.
- It is predictable, consistent, and kind: students know what is expected, work proceeds at a pace that aligns with competence, and is collaborative rather than competitive.

How to Do it

The traditional rubric that is supposed to "help" learners is designed by adults who are easily able to manage two or more concepts: Exceeding, Meeting, Approaching, and Below standards. When children see these concepts, at least 50% of children will recognize themselves through their reticular activating system (RAS) as Below or Approaching, no matter how much effort goes into teaching.

Instead, reduce the structure down to one column: Exceeding Standards. This alerts their RAS to strive towards Exceeding.

💡 School is fun when we gain mastery through Agency.

Dysfunction

The brain is primal and attuned to survival. So, it's no surprise that children get lost in a reactive behavior that is contrary to school rules and human social "norms."

When the adult inquires, "What were you thinking? Why did you set fire to James' hair?" the response will invariably be dumbfounded, "I don't know."

The truth is, the child likely doesn't know. When the amygdala cuts off access to the rational higher-order thinking brain, all kinds of strange outcomes can occur.

It is at moments like this that as adults, we need to step back, take a deep breath or two, and become curious. "I wonder, what is going on in this child's life that is causing this outbreak and escalation?"

When the teacher remains curious, they will be able to avoid the contagion of the reactive outburst. Two people in an amygdala hijack is a recipe for disaster.

What's Really Happening?

Incoming sensory information is processed based on what type of information it is, and what is already going on in the amygdala:

a. Visual (sight) and auditory (sound) are first processed by the **Thalamus.** It gets sent to the amygdala or directly to the cortex.
b. Olfactory (smell) and tactile (touch) bypass the Thalamus and go directly to the **Amygdala**.

Depending on how active the child's amygdala is, incoming sensory information is either sent to the frontal cortex for processing in a rational way (normal activity), or sent to the hindbrain (hyperactivity). It is the intentional activity of the neural informed educator to create environments that allow the reasoning "rational" brain gain access to incoming sensory information for processing and meaning-making.

The Rhythmic Envelope

Including music or rhythmic activities in your classroom helps eliminate stress and competition (for most children) and sets the stage for learning.

Rhythm is associated with the brain's **Basal Ganglia**. In particular, with the **Putamen** – an important region that supports learning and motor control. Among other things, it manages speech articulation, language functions, reward, and cognitive regulation.

Regulation teaches children how to inhibit certain drives and instincts, and how to engage in social activities in a positive way. By growing structures in areas that connect the hippocampus, amygdala, and frontal lobe processing, the teacher can first co-regulate, so they will soon be able to self-regulate.

Finally, relationships are critical in the learning process. Relationship-building helps a child feel a sense of belonging and safety, which are critical precursors to learning.

How to Do it

1. Activities that are encapsulated in a "rhythmic envelope" invite rhythm, regulation, and relationship-building into your classroom.

2. Create a rhythmic envelope by playing with rhythm in the classroom. Bring in some high-energy rhythm music and invite the children to move or beat drums to the music.

3. Combine breathing practices with rhythmic activities through music. This helps reduce activity in the amygdala and restore order in the child's brain.

💡 Rhythm, regulation, and relationship make learning fun for all children.

Stuck With the Contagious 3 P's

Mom is exasperated. She is examining the blank paper where the school project should be near finished. "How come you haven't even begun? You have known about it for three weeks! I don't understand… it's not even hard. You can do this without even thinking. It makes no sense."

Her young son is also frustrated. It's due tomorrow and he hasn't even started yet. It's going to be a disaster. "I hate school," he thinks to himself. "I hate these English essays," he blurts out by way of explanation. But mom is not buying it.

"When you were younger, you never missed an assignment. What's going on?"

In truth, he doesn't know. He has a jumpy feeling in his belly and he feels nauseated. "I don't feel well." Again, his mom is not accepting this.

"You haven't even written down the title. What's the title of this project? You have been staring at it all week." Geeesh!

What's Really Happening?

Mom is right. Her son should be able to do this simple assignment. Why is it so difficult for some children to commit to writing an essay? For many children, this all starts with the first of three P's: **Perfection**. He knows the material and he has a vision for what it might look like in his essay. He can already hear the applause at the end. But, he realizes that the initial draft will be very meager, even dowdy. So, he waits until it will be better. Time passes while his *waiting* drags on. This triggers the second of the three P's: **Procrastination**. Suddenly, three weeks have passed. He is still thinking about his brilliant project and sees himself getting a great score. But the pressure of time running out introduces the last of the three P's: **Paralysis**.

Get Unstuck From the Contagious 3 P's

Another student, Marjorie, laughs as she writes her essay. Marjorie began her essay the day that the project was assigned. She is using the scaffold that her class uses with easy-to-follow information.

Her first draft is not great, but it is a great start. She realizes that she needs help with the summary and the conclusion. So she wrote a note and brought it to her teacher the next day.

Having seen how easy it was to get a good grade with this method, Marjorie knew what to do next time.

Benefits

- There are no right or wrong answers.
- It's an iterative process that can be used again and again with better results each time.

How to Do it

1. Avoid the amygdala hijack caused by **Perfectionism** by giving children opportunities to make lots of mistakes in the Phonological Loop.
2. Instead of giving a long window to turn in materials, give smaller tasks and shorter timeframes (i.e. write the intro by tomorrow). This leaves no time for **Procrastination**.
3. As the student learns mastery with these scaffolds, the serotonin, dopamine, and oxytocin their brain releases, act as a barrier to **Paralysis**.

💡 The Phonological Loop is a connection between Broca's and Wernicke's Areas that facilitate reading.

Calm Down!

"If I have told you once, I have told you a million times, STOP that obnoxious whining, and knuckle down to your work." Even the most patient teacher at times feels like screaming at the children. Do you ever feel this way?

I hate when I lose my cool. I feel awful when I have to discipline a child and cause them to lose recess, or "Free Dress Friday", or sometimes have them expelled for more serious transgressions. There are rules... there are Zero Tolerance policies which I have to abide by... I don't see any other way!

If only they were ready for learning - there is so much value in the information that I have for these children. I didn't become a teacher to scream at children, nor for that matter, to punish children for their behavior which is disruptive and interferes with other children's ability to participate.

What's Really Happening?

The amygdala hijack is contagious. The last thing that should happen in any school is a teacher in an amygdala hijack, at the same time that a child is in an amygdala hijack. There are times when the teacher can feel that their buttons are being pressed, that the student is deliberately provoking them and that the only solution is to pull rank and revert to discipline policies.

If the child is in a provoking, reactive, disruptive mindset, it is already too late. No matter how much discipline, no matter how much screaming or shouting, the child will be unable to move beyond the involuntary reaction that is a response to the crisis that is causing the brain reaction. The teacher, as the adult in the room, must be armed with the knowledge and neural lens that can de-escalate the reaction before it gets way out of control.

Are You OK?

From the first day in school, introduce the child to their brain. In particular, teach about the almond-shaped amygdala so that they have the vocabulary to build mental models about what happens when the amygdala is hijacked and they lose access to their rational thinking brain.

Then, give children this intentional cognitive rehearsal exercise so they can myelinate the structures that highlight the effect of anger, fear, resentment, and other emotions.

Benefits

- This exercise uses mirror neuron techniques to help the child de-escalate.
- The child connects their cerebellum and occipital brain with the limbic brain (amygdala).
- The child learns and practices how to cope with difficult emotional challenges that prepare them for life.

How to Do it

1. Use a ball or two to help focus a distraught child with some physical activities while you breathe visibly and audibly.
2. Pass the ball back and forth, or roll the ball across the floor to one another as you talk about what's bothering the child.
3. When the child has regained composure, plan a follow-up role-playing event where the child teaches other children what it means to "survive" amygdala hijack.

💡 Begin by being curious. When one is curious, one cannot be angry at the same time.

The Perils of Punishment

In theory, one would think that a reward system would always work in school. Children who are compliant and who turn their work in on time get rewarded. Children who are disruptive, not following instructions, saying or doing inappropriate things at inappropriate times get punished. Either they are given something undesirable (like detention or extra work), or they miss out on something (a pizza party or Fun Friday).

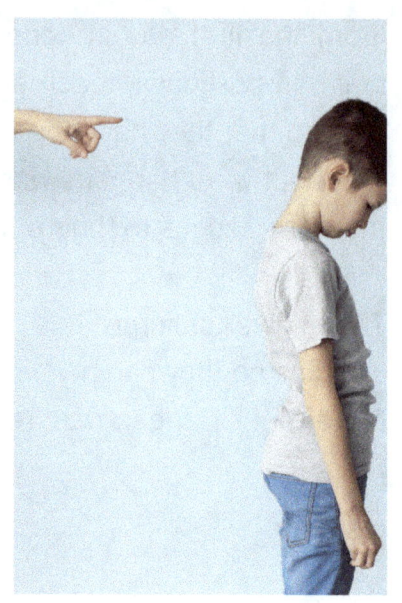

Such behavior modification programs are designed to bring children's behavior into line with school discipline plans or classroom management systems. So why don't they work? Why do some children continue to misbehave despite the punishments?

What's Really Happening?

Poorly sourced behavioral plans rarely work because children who struggle to fit in, learn to mask their ineptitude with defense mechanisms that allow them to participate somewhat until they either drop out, or squeeze through. Either way, these children fail to reach their full potential. This is a blot on a school's reputation and especially painful for teachers who realize that they were not able to build a meaningful relationship with some children. Most teachers are interested in their students being able to survive and also thrive in school.

Public shaming like labeling, stratification, and competitive learning systems are invariably meaningless for children who show high autonomic nervous system reactivity. These "Orchid" kids will respond negatively to anything that they perceive as dangerous, competitive, or stressful. Even the most well-meaning intervention that is designed around token economies, rewards or punishments, will be outside the zone of proximal development for the child who is anxious, sad, resentful, or alone.

All the Children Get All the Joy

All children are able to learn. However, children will thrive in the learning space if they can. And all children want to learn. In order for every child to feel like they can learn, it is incumbent on the teacher to adjust the environment so that the child is able to learn.

Instead of punishing an entire group because one child was not able to finish the project on time, or able to stay quiet in the line, it makes more sense to give joy to all the children. The child who is struggling will learn a lot more from the sense of belonging, the shared oxytocin, and the joy of being included in school, than a punishment.

Benefits

- Every child benefits when every child is included.
- The child who is afraid will be comforted.
- The child who is lonely will make friends.

How to Do it

1. Focus your teaching around joy. No more veiled threats and punishments, especially not public shaming.
2. Stay childlike in your curiosity. Why might a particular child not be able to access the joy in school or in learning?
3. Begin the week with dopamine, oxytocin and serotonin with Magic Monday, rather than holding out for Fun Friday. Everyday can be a fun learning day.

💡 What works for the child who needs that extra scaffold, will work for all the children.

I'm Angry

Anger is common, but there are so many different kinds of "angry" that it's difficult even to comprehend how angry a child is at any one time.

The bigger problem derives from the fact that children typically do not have the vocabulary to describe how they feel other than "angry."

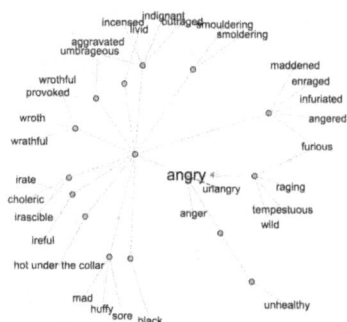

However, a quick look at the word "angry" from the **Visual Thesaurus** site, will highlight 50 words that refer to the most onerous of sentiments that can cause so much crisis in classrooms. From this interactive map, children can step into a world that defines the intensity of their feeling in much greater nuance and depth so that it is easy to measure the size of the reaction.

When a child is in the moment of reactive response, it is easy to catastrophize the problem, to see it as overbearing and huge. However, when we can step back and take a breath, the child has an opportunity to find a word that fits the "right size" of their emotion and the issue that caused the outburst.

What's Really Happening?

When we have only one word for a feeling, an emotion, or a sentiment, there is no opportunity to compare and contrast. There is a big difference between the meanings of the following words: upset, sad, indignant, livid, furious, or enraged.

A child who has only one word to express this range of emotion is less able to visualize a way out. In fact, over time the child can talk or think themselves into a bigger, deeper emotional reaction because there is no yardstick to visualize the internal hurt.

This inability to regulate oneself in transient emotional states feeds a downward negative spiral. This, in turn, can contribute more ammunition to the RAS filter, which is often seeking more reasons to confirm low self-esteem and lack of efficacy.

What's Below Anger

Hidden below anger can be a seething morass of feelings and emotions that are hard to label. Any work we do with children in this space should include new vocabulary that illuminates the feeling and nails it to a word.

For instance, instead of being angry, the child might feel tricked, embarrassed, frustrated, frightened, rejected, guilty, hungry, lonely, tired, abandoned, envious, disappointed, regretful, overwhelmed, worried, nervous – or a combination of any or all these emotions.

It begins with words. Vocabulary is a roadmap to mental models, and from there to deep understanding. Very soon a child will be able to help another child when they ask the all-important question: "Are you angry or just lonely?"

Self-regulation thrives on co-regulation. Co-create the emotional stage with the student by allowing them to process powerful emotions about how they feel in regard to real-life issues that are in their world (e.g. *"I am sad because my puppy is very sick."*)

How to Do it

1. Use a thesaurus and dictionary to play with "emotion" words in the phonological loop.
2. Co-create a visual continuum with word cards where children can see and move the emotion along a continuum from "not too bad" to "very serious."
3. After an emotional outburst, revisit the emotion to add vocabulary that "right-sizes" it.

💡 Emotion mapping is an easy way to anchor a child's understanding of a wide range of emotions to real-world situations.

Behavior Is...

Most teachers view behavior as either compliant or not compliant. But we have come up with many different descriptions of behavior to define children, rather than their behaviors, and what is going on in the brain.

For instance, teachers can easily make sense of the many descriptors that connect with unacceptable classroom interactions. Children tend to get labeled as "high fliers" when they seem aggressive, attention-seeking, or take up inordinate amounts of energy and time. Here are more common labels that often categorize some children in learning spaces:

- Troublesome, Out-of-Control
- Insolent, Defiant
- Rude, Disrespectful
- Oppositional, Aggressive
- Unruly, Disruptive

What's Really Happening?

There is no doubt that children can be troubled, troublesome, insolent, rude, aggressive, and disruptive. But when we look at their developmental curve from a neuroscientific lens, we realize they are exactly where they are supposed to be. Children aren't born with regulation in place. It is important to realize that regulation (and self-regulation in particular) is a learned skill. It is defined by a particular series of specialized neural circuits that connect the occipital, temporal, parietal, and frontal lobes. It is the job of the adults in the child's life – the parents and teachers – to help them build important neuronal structures that prepare the child for adult life and interaction in society.

Communication

When you know the science of the amygdala hijack, of mirror neurons, and practice self-regulation yourself, you can best show up as the expert when a child needs guidance.

All children will at some point in their school career get into a scrape where they will react and do, or say, something that appears out of character. This is good. All children need to know what an amygdala hijack feels like in a safe learning environment. School is that place.

Sure, it is going to disturb the math class or the language lesson, but we are not only teaching content, we are also teaching children. One of the greatest gifts we can impart to any child is the ability to recognize and recover from a very difficult amygdala hijack. They might already have enough to contend with.

"I don't understand this material. I don't want my friends to think I am dumb."
"The police took my dad away yesterday."
"My parents were fighting. I got no sleep last night."

How to Do it

1. Disruptive or aggressive behavior is to be expected. Plan for it, rather than fight against it, to give children the opportunity to learn and grow in this space.
2. Instead of raising your voice to yell "Calm down," or "Don't do that!" remain calm and use mirror neuron interventions like deep breathing to allow space for recovery.
3. When the amygdala hijack is over, invite the student to teach what amygdala hijack feels like to peers, with role-play outcomes that are good or bad.

💡 Behavior is simply communication, and all behavior is defined by a neural substrate.

2 x 4

In a behaviorist, extrinsic world, there are few choices when it comes to motivating children. We were taught that teaching children to repeat behaviors that are perceived as *good* requires praise and/or rewards (a carrot).

Similarly, we were trained to punish children who misbehave (or act with "unexpected" behavior that disrupts classroom activities), to change their approach to learning. In fact, most school systems have very carefully drawn up policies (e.g. Zero Tolerance) that define a teacher's options for managing such instances. This was the stick analogy.

In the old days, the carrot and stick mentality was accompanied by physical rewards and punishments; children got food for doing good things or got beaten with a leather or a cane for transgressing. Colloquially, this latter method was referred to as a "two-by-four" persuasion.

What's Really Happening?

We now know that rewards and punishments don't work. Roughly 50% of children respond equally to rewards and punishments. Resilient children (referred here to as **dandelinic**) bounced back easily and were minimally affected by threats, punishments, or words. Equally, rewards failed to impress them. Threats or rewards didn't elicit the groundbreaking outcomes that we expected.

The other 50% of children in the class were not quite as easily understood. Neither rewards nor punishments caused them to change their behavior. In fact, their disruptive, oppositional activities seemed to persist in spite of the painful interventions that we had at our disposal.

It turns out that **"orchidial"** learners do not react favorably to either rewards or punishments.

2 x 10

Instead of punishing children, try a different approach. Try to not have grades be the focus of learning. When a teacher is intentional and deliberate about building a strong positive relationship with a child, amazing outcomes are the result — behaviorally, academically, and socially.

For school to feel safe and fun for children who are less resilient and more sensitive to social context, teachers must be: Predictable, Consistent, and Kind.

In addition, school itself needs to be predictable, consistent, and kind. In other words, no grades, no spot quizzes, no double standards, no homework.

Instead, try the **"Two by Ten"** method of relationship building.

How to Do it

1. Be intentional about meeting every child for just 2 minutes each day for 10 days at a specific place and time.

2. Listen to the child, hear what they have to say and what is causing them worry.

3. Let the child know that it is your job to help them be successful and grades or difficult concepts can be accomplished without fear over time together.

💡 All children have unspoken fears and anxieties that are very real to them. Negative thinking impacts on their ability to focus, pay attention and their readiness to build relationships and learn.

Section II: Relate

Children are not broken. It's not that children learn if they want to. Children learn when they can. They DO want to! We accomplish this NOT by attempting to change the child. We simply change the environment. What is getting in the way? Remove the barriers so that all students can access learning.

– Tabitha Ellison, M.Ed

Alive 'til Twenty-Five

One death every eleven minutes. These are difficult statistics to accept. Data from CDC confirm that suicides are on the rise in a post-pandemic, chaotic world. And sadly, these numbers are increasing in younger and younger ages.

Suicide affects people of all ages, but there's reason to be concerned at the high prevalence of suicide in school-age children. In 2020, suicide was among the top 9 leading causes of death for people aged 10-64. It was also the second leading cause of death for children aged 10-14 and young adults aged 25-34. To stop child suicide, we must think differently about getting our children through school and adolescence. We have to adjust to the changing world in which we find ourselves.

Keep them alive until 25 is not just peculiar to fragile parents; it's already a social construct. As parents of teens, we are familiar with how insurers view "risk" associated with children as they step into the automobile world at ages closer to 16 than 25. Now, we need to consider – and reduce – the risk of suicide as well.

Consider this: A baby zebra has to be prepared to get up, stand steady, walk and run fast within minutes of finding itself dropped onto a hard savanna plain. So, why is it that some species are born with the capacity to survive and thrive almost immediately, while in our advanced *Homo sapiens* world, it can take up to 25 years for a child to reach maturity? *Homo sapiens*, with its preponderance of neurons in the frontal lobe (a lot more than Neanderthals, and twice more than chimpanzees and bonobos), need that extra time to connect and myelinate white-matter tracts that reflect experience and environment. There is nothing magical about the age 25, except that as adolescents reach for identity, find their place in the world, and gain experience by contributing, we know that their amazing malleable brains are working with and for them.

Therefore, it is the teacher's job (*in loco parentis*) to help build and link these important white matter structures, so that the child will be able to engage in its life and journey. What does it mean to build white matter structures? Most teachers have never been taught to think about white matter structures, and if they *are* familiar with one in particular, it is probably the **corpus callosum**. Beyond connecting the left and right hemispheres, they are more likely not aware of other advantages that a well-formed corpus callosum can provide for their students.

There are many other white matter structures that are critical in the learning space. In the following pages, we will highlight these and indicate advantages that show up in the classroom by implementing methods that are informed by neuroscience.

Structures, Relationships, and Fun

Brains connect through growing white matter tracts in and between lobes. This begins at the back and reaches out to all other regions and eventually to the front. Parents and teachers share a goal to help a child architect a well-connected brain so that the child grows up to find meaning in the world.

The brand-new infant begins to make connections with the world outside the womb as soon as it is born. At the back of the brain, the **Cerebellum** (Latin for "Little Brain") is situated just above the brainstem and basically defines the infant's innate abilities. The cerebellum is the fastest-growing brain region in the child's life. By three months, it will have doubled in volume. We can easily appreciate this development, simply by observing the child's emerging abilities to engage with its surroundings, signal to caregivers its needs and learning, and even indicate displeasures. Even though this "little" brain is much smaller than the rest of the infant's brain, this is where most of the neurons reside.

The brainstem and the cerebellum comprise the child's reptilian survival brain. This means that the child has a very early formed and solidly developed instinct for survival and staying alive. When you are up feeding and caring for the infant at 3:00 am, you understand that the child's needs for survival are pivotal.

So, what does this mean for the teacher in the classroom? Children like to move – to swing, to roll, to jump, and so on – so activating the cerebellum should be a central part of classroom activities. A teacher preparing a lesson plan for preschoolers, kindergarten, and so on, should wonder, "Where am I engaging with the child's cerebellum in this lesson?"

When a child is bouncing on a trampoline at the same time as learning to spell long words, not only are they playing in the phonological loop, they are also growing structures from the cerebellum to the occipital, the temporal, the parietal, and the prefrontal cortex. Teachers are also aware that elementary, middle school, and high school children are more apt to engage, more ready to generate ideas, and more willing to collaborate and contribute when the cerebellum is introduced during instruction and relationship building in preteen and teenage years.

Invisible Plan

"Why were you so rough on your friend Jaden?" The teacher was trying to prevent the two boys from getting hurt, and from getting into even deeper trouble.

"Well, he won't pass the ball to me... he never passes to anyone." Sammy was sweating and heated as well.

"I will, but first I wanted to try out that new move that we learned, the Cruyff Turn. Then I will pass it to you." Jaden was frustrated. Why didn't Sammy just wait a bit longer?

"That sounds like fun. What's a Cruyff Turn?" The teacher was genuinely interested in knowing this soccer move.

Jaden proceeded to demonstrate as best he could, but it didn't turn out that clean. He managed to turn the ball, but he tripped himself up and both boys laughed. "Let me have a try." Sammy was all in.

What's Really Happening?

All children have plans and dreams. When the plan or dream is unspoken, the student and the consequential behavior can remain an enigma for everyone else. When a teacher's plan differs from a student's plan, unexpected behavior can be the outcome. Arguments and misunderstandings can be avoided if we help children voice their invisible plans.

Making visible is a valuable and very important part of the teacher's skill set. The children will not be aware of the process, but when their thinking is made visible, then it is possible to understand their behavior, determine how tightly fused they are to the plan, and figure out a transition for moving on to a plan that works for everyone.

I Wish My Teacher Knew...

Children have plans and dreams that might not be so easily made visible because they come from a different part of the brain. These dreams are often deep-rooted in identity, personality and cultural mores and may not be readily accessible to either teacher or peers.

The exercise, "I Wish My Teacher Knew…." is a simple and private way for children to make visible their worries, doubts, and fears.

Benefits

- Teacher-child relationships deepen.
- The child realizes that their dream is real and meaningful.
- Children learn that it's okay to be part of the herd, each contribution is important.

How to Do it

1. On a 4 x 6 card, write the phrase "I wish my teacher knew…"
2. Give the card to the child to finish the sentence, using words or drawings to tell their story.
3. Review the card and open a conversation to help the child see that you understand and are there to support them in their worry, dream, or plan.

💡 Try this exercise anonymously if children are afraid or embarrassed to participate.

Screaming & Kicking

It happens every morning. It's time for school, but mommy's little girl is not happy. She is causing quite a ruckus, screaming and kicking. She can do this for hours. The upset child is somewhat contained while mommy is still in the vicinity, but as soon as mommy leaves she quickly disintegrates into an unmanageable puddle of tears. This behavior is ultra-contagious and affects everyone in the room.

Why is it that some children seem to handle separation anxiety and increased mental stressors with ease, while others just seem to lack any resilience?

It boils down to just that. *Some children are hardwired to be more resilient; some are less so.*

In every family, it becomes clear over time that one child is "easy" to raise, while another is anything but. Parents pick up on just how sensitive that particular child is; they need extra caring, don't conform as readily as the other siblings and are often at the emergency room with earaches, scratches, allergies, and more.

What's Really Happening?

Children pick up on their parents' body language. Voice changes from the parent signal their own increased separation anxiety since many parents are anxious for their child's first tentative steps into the learning world. "I don't want to go to school," screams the child, while mommy is trying to balance work, home, and a dysregulated child.

Children do not have a well-developed notion of time. They cannot predict how long mommy will be missing. The overarching anxiety has to do with the fact that "Mommy goed!" Fear, anxiety, stress, and loneliness combine to kick the child into **amygdala hijack** – a survival reaction that shuts down the child's capacity to access their prefrontal cortex. Other children or an adult teacher may add to the confusion and increase stress.

Transitions can be Predictable

Every child's brain processes incoming sensory information in similar ways. When the child's parents and teachers understand how the child's brain works, they will be in a better position to manage trauma that is onset by separation, anxiety, and stressors that show up in life.

The first day of school is but one of those novel situations that cause the brain to react, because evolutionary hardwired systems kick into action to safeguard and protect the child. It is a sad truism that modern life, along with culture and norms, moves at a much quicker pace than biological evolution.

The child is governed primarily by constraints that have been working for millions of years of evolution — systems that are designed for survival. Rather than create a threat response with unpredictability, we can create a space that puts the promise of survival first, followed by secondary emotional feelings, and eventually by tertiary rational thoughts. How? By being *predictable, consistent and kind* in our thoughts and actions.

How to Do it

1. **Be predictable:** A child's brain loves predictability, so set up systems daily that are predictable, especially when we know that transitions are necessary.
2. **Be consistent:** Set up systems daily that meet the child's needs with regard to consistent flow, consistent smells, and consistent feelings.
3. **Be kind:** Set up systems in which the adult acts kindly (which is vital), but the environment is also kind.

💡 Children thrive when the teacher and environment is predictable, consistent and kind.

Threats Stop Learning

There are many types of threats that can interfere with a child's ability to learn. Some are physical, some are social, and others are unintended but real. While schools work hard to curtail and avoid physical and social threats, hidden unintended threats are universal, persistent, and silent.

Every child is motivated to preserve their social self. That means maintaining social esteem, status, and value. There is nothing as effective as destroying the social self as getting a bad grade on a test or performing in front of people who are judging.

Research shows that stressors (like testing) derived from social evaluation and uncontrollability, cause large increases in cortisol in children. The same tasks that children undertake without social evaluation or lack of controllability do not elicit the cortisol response. School need not be so detrimental to learning for kids.

What's Really Happening?

Children who are naturally resilient will breeze through all kinds of stressors. Evidence from research in areas that measure children's autonomic nervous system reactivity shows that Social Evaluative Threat has less of an impact on these resilient learners.

At the same time, children who describe high levels of autonomic nervous system reactivity are less resilient and highly influenced by **Social Evaluative Threat**. Many teachers have never even heard of Social Evaluative Threat and, therefore, are not looking out for signs of it in their children's behavior.

We know that high levels of cortisol cause that icky feeling in the belly. Children will often ask to go to the nurse, or to the bathroom, or to go home with a pain in the tummy. Other children will experience *freeze* symptoms.

Sense of Belonging Enhances Learning

Social Evaluative Threat will prevent a child from being able to demonstrate competence. Thankfully, all children love to learn and the Social Evaluative Threat is easy to recognize and fix.

All children thrive when they have an opportunity to originate new ideas, valuable thoughts, and concrete items that are meaningful for the classroom and peers.

It is easy to be intentional about creating a learning space that welcomes a child's individual creativity, without any mention of rewards or punishments.

How to Do it

1. Focus on praising the effort, not the child. Instead of saying "great work, Peter," highlight the fact that Peter put a lot of *effort* into the work and didn't give up when obstacles presented themselves. For example: "I'm so proud that you took a deep breath and persisted in the face of setbacks."

2. Design your activities to allow children to experience autonomy and a contagious sense of belonging at school. Introduce fun activities that guarantee oxytocin and serotonin in the learning space so that the child is able to generate new ideas and contribute to the work of others.

3. Be mindful of the child's emotional needs. Respond with hands-on tangibles that highlight security, happiness with peers, and solid connection to the child's caring adults.

💡 By maintaining a clear connection to intrinsic motivation, the child will experience Mastery that feeds into a sense of Purpose.

Can't Breathe

Marjorie was usually a "good" kid, but every now and then she found herself at the principal's office. The principal always said the same thing to her: "I'm a little surprised to find you here, Marjorie. You are usually a well-behaved student."

Marjorie gazed wide-eyed at Mrs. Johnson. "I'm kinda surprised too. I don't usually get that upset in class."

It started with Facebook. How could her BFF unfriend her, over something so simple? It was the last straw. Marjorie lost it in English Language Arts. By the time she arrived at Mrs. Johnson's office, she was hot, angry, and sad. Her mouth felt dry. Mrs. Johnson took a long deep breath.

"I can't breathe," Marjorie panicked. Mrs. Johnson was really calm. She stood quietly and took another long deep breath. Her office was a mess, bags of stuff thrown everywhere after the PTO Fundraiser last night. Her eye fell on the broken plastic shopping bag that was losing bits of jewelry that hadn't even been sorted yet. She emptied it in one big clump on the table.

"Can you help me organize this jewelry?"

What's Really Happening?

Marjorie was experiencing a classic **amygdala hijack**. Being unable to breathe was part of her stress reaction. Mrs. Johnson was the adult in the room, recognized the crisis, and immediately used a simple strategy to connect her neurons with Marjorie's. Deep breathing and **mirroring** defused the situation. Mirror neurons are a surefire way to connect with a brain that is experiencing stress and coping with behavior that is oppositional and reactive. Marjorie was able to take a breath, shallow at first, but soon deeper and more relieving. Her mouth didn't feel so dry anymore. The amygdala hijack was diffusing.

Relate with Jewelry

During an amygdala hijack, an individual might not be able to access a rational response. Don't let this throw you off – the adult in the room cannot afford to experience an amygdala hijack also.

Using a strategy like organizing jewelry, can help you co-regulate with small motor skills and simple cognitive skills at the same time.

For Marjorie, messed-up jewelry intrigued her. One by one she was able to separate the pieces and make complementary pairings with earrings, bracelets, and hair slides. She was soon able to face her Facebook crisis with a calm, cool, rational brain.

How to Do it

1. Learn to identify when a child is in amygdala hijack: The child will experience a racing heart beat; sweaty palms; won't be able to think clearly; difficulty with logic; emotional outbursts; embarrassed afterwards.

2. Keep an assortment of old jewelry in a large box to use whenever a student experiences cognitive impairment due to amygdala hijack. Introduce other kinetic tangibles also - kinetic sand, mini sand box to rake, fidget puzzles, things to stack, other items like the jewelry to sort on hand.

3. Introducing a repetitive cognitive task that includes small motor movements helps bypass the amygdala and put the rational brain back in control.

💡 De-escalation is easy as long as the adult in the room stays calm and refuses to be dragged into a reactive amygdala hijack too.

Can't Think

Working memory is so miniscule that it doesn't take much to fill it. And when it's full, it's full. The thing is, you, as teacher, didn't say or do anything that caused the child's working memory to be full.

The child shows up in your classroom and by all appearances is ready to learn. However, unknown to you or anyone else, that child is still processing something negative, something harmful, something hurtful that occurred in some other place at some other time.

It seems impossible to reach this child because even though they are sitting in the classroom right here, right now, they are in some other place in their head. They are therefore not present.

What's Really Happening?

The child's working memory is small. Imagine the difference between all the grains of sand on all the beaches on the planet, versus your coffee cup. That cup is tiny by comparison to the grains of sand, or all the stars in the Milky Way. This is the same as comparing the capacity of the child's brain versus the child's **working memory**. It's important to know that a child's brain has an immense capacity, which is limited by an hour-glass shaped gateway called working memory.

Working Memory fills in a flash - teachers experience this also. Something that was said or not said, something that reminded them of something bad, harmful, or hurtful... fills it.

Yet, as teachers, we have to pass through that minuscule hourglass-like space called Working Memory to get to the thinking brain. As educators, if we are able to help children clear their working memory from negative information, we can have much more success in activating their learning and problem solving.

Mirror with Peer

Mirror neurons are the perfect antidote to many overload crises that happen in the child's brain. When there is no more room in working memory, the child might cycle down into negative territory. This is the time to relate to the child… a story that lets them feel that they are not alone. Your mirror neurons talk to their mirror neurons in a supportive, happy way.

Mirror neurons are sensory motor cells that react when a particular action is performed by someone nearby, or when it is observed by the child who is looking for relatedness. In other words, we *mirror* other's actions.

Neuroscientists believe that the neural basis for empathy may be a system of mirror neurons.

We all escalate from time to time. And we all appreciate a chance to de-escalate with mirror neurons.

How to Do it

You can use this mirror system to engage the child at a primal level and work carefully to de-escalate elevated moods and reactions. It's as easy as simply breathing or walking together.

1. Begin by taking deep loud breaths in the vicinity of the child who is experiencing cognitive overload.

2. When the child is able and willing, go for a walk together in a quiet peaceful place (preferably outside). As you walk, intentionally copy their gait and hand motion.

3. Note: It is important not to raise your voice or change your body language while using mirror neurons, as these may escalate the situation.

💡 It is easy to help children think when you use mirror neurons to clear working memory.

Dandelinic Compliance

It seems counterintuitive, but powerful learning can happen even if there is no trace of compliance. Very often, we find agency and a sense of belonging in a chaotic co-created learning space.

It's hard to justify it without knowing the teacher or the students, but I'm happy to go out on a limb from past experience, to state that a quiet structured class is not necessarily the ideal learning environment.

Some children find it difficult to concentrate and focus when there is too much noise. Indeed there are times when quiet, focused schoolwork makes sense. However, much of the momentum for agency, engagement, generating novel ideas, and asking incisive questions, derives from spaces where children are able to step outside their comfort zones, take risks, and challenge each other in productive small-group interactions.

What's Really Happening?

When the classroom is structured so that silence and compliance is equated with learning, many children are left out. In particular, sensitive thinkers are easily distracted in a space where overt competitive practice pegs one child against the other. In an intense survival space like this, many children will give up easily and choose not to persist to defy the odds of success.

Many learning spaces that are designed to be competitive (intentionally or by default) end up being so extrinsic that the true purpose of the teacher's intent is masked by winner-takes-all thinking. There can only be one winner in such a system. There's one winner, and the rest of the students can easily see themselves as losers.

A safe learning space makes room for voice, personality, and emotional connection so that every child has an opportunity to participate, in particular an opportunity to contribute.

Orchidial Chaos

We each show up in society as a consequence of our hardwired genetic gifts. Instead of focusing on curricular content, and delivering lessons in an efficient structured way, try *front-loading* for fun. This means engaging interplay with active social engagement.

In order to understand the complexity of a group of learners, we need to understand an individual's "Differential Neurobiological Susceptibility to Social Context." Simply speaking, this means that a child will show up in any social context hard-wired to react based on their genetic expression. It turns out that the social setting is the agent that expresses the genetic outcome.

Every child will need:
   a. A sense of belonging
   b. Trust
   c. Friendship
   d. Safety (physical and psychological)
   e. Me Here Now

How to Do it

1. Create a greenhouse in your classroom by inviting each learner to feel safe in the social context of the learning space. Focus on the work that demonstrates progress over competition.

2. Adjust the social context (the environment) instead of changing the child (with rewards or punishments) for best engagement and incremental academic output.

3. The child will find their own greenhouse by default. If it is not in your classroom, your school, or their home, it will unfortunately be in some less safe place or circumstance.

💡 Remember to be *kind*. Choose thoughtfully those red marks when giving feedback.

Managing Classrooms

We have all spent thousands of hours in traditional classrooms. We recognize them immediately – they haven't changed much since Aristotle's day. A teacher stands in front of children who are usually sitting in rows. Success correlates easily with compliant engagement.

Efficiency and economy are still important features of school, but a quick visit to most schools would show a very different picture. In every school in any country, there are children who are not able to keep up. Sometimes they start with a deficit in preparatory foundational skills. These tend to get worse over time and in spite of well-meaning interventions, these same children often struggle until they give up and drop out.

The teacher is forced to spend an inordinate amount of time and resources managing children in often chaotic classrooms.

What's Really Happening?

In that model of school, there is an implicit element of competition. Learners are rewarded for engaging and being eager to contribute. This should work in theory, but the hard reality is that children learn to *survive* in these pressure zones. Here, punishments are distributed every day in relation to a child's ability to keep up, pay attention, or hide below the teacher's radar. While most schools profess to be "child-centric", we know that school focus is always on discipline, grades, and attempts to fill children with enough knowledge so that they will achieve academic standards according to a remote high-stakes test.

And for the teacher, life is very different from what they envisioned when they took the job in order to change the world. Instead, they find themselves administering token economies, stars, grades, and other rewards or, on the other hand, punishing children for their inability to compete and stay up with the scope and sequence.

Managing Brains

In the past, we didn't have access to instruments or information that illuminated what was going on inside the child's brain as they learned. Thankfully, that is no longer the case today.

To create a cognitive learning space, we focus less on content and more on the children. Rather than forcing children to memorize, we use content like math and science to build the child's ability to think.

Benefits

- The child learns to self-regulate.
- The child is able to think critically.
- The child is prepared for future learning.

How to Do it

1. Begin with words. Use vocabulary that relates to the neuroscience of learning to build mental models that grow structures and myelinate synaptic connections.

    Example: Say "oxytocin" instead of "behavior." Replace constructs like "good" with "dopamine" and "serotonin" and "amygdala hijack", instead of "bad behavior" or "outburst." Stay as positive when speaking about children as possible. 💡 Remember to be *kind*. Choose thoughtfully those red marks when giving feedback.

2. Co-create a learning space rather than always leading. This makes children feel part of their learning experience, welcome, and capable.

💡 You don't have to change everything about your curriculum, a few simple tweaks can lead to remarkable successes.

Teacher Shouldn't Be Busy

I used to spend hours, even days preparing my classroom so that it was "perfect" for my students when they showed up on day one.

I believed a classroom should be neat, it should have all the items I would need to manage the class, it should have my stuff safe from paws that might interfere with it, and it should have the daily do's clearly on display so that everyone knew what was going on, and so on.

I later realized this setup was sabotaging me:

1. I was doing all the work.
2. I was still not getting the results I sought.
3. I owned the classroom – it was MY class.

It never dawned upon me that the children didn't see it as their class, too. They referred to it as Mr. O's classroom. Equally, it never dawned upon me that I was protective of the decor and the space. When things weren't where they *should be*, I got upset.

What's Really Happening?

I was consumed with my own idea of what an ideal classroom *should* look like, and what *should* happen in an ideal classroom. The sad reality was that I was not successful in achieving these goals, despite the work I put into my classroom. The children didn't have any commitment to this classroom and its decorative fixtures. Plus, I was doing all the work and I was exhausted.

In effect, the children had to learn to feel safe in *my* space every time they entered the room. How much of their working memory was consumed with issues that had nothing to do with the content of my lesson? How much of their working memory was consumed with feeling part of the community? I could fix this.

Children Should Be Busy

I learned a lot the first year that I stepped away from designing the "best" classroom ever. Instead of a completed classroom, I introduced the children on the first day to a project that we would all have to apply ourselves to, in order to have a functioning room. For weeks afterward, I discovered that the children came up with plans for additions and changes that were meaningful and inclusive.

The difference was that it was *their* room. They were excited to get involved each new day with plans that made their room safer and more welcoming for everyone.

When people came to *their* classroom they were the ones to welcome them into their space. It was a safe space where they saw themselves in it for all kinds of academic and social items that had real value to them.

The children were proud to manage their classroom all year and excited to show their talent and genius.

How to Do it

1. Rather than decorate your classroom alone, invite your students to co-create their learning space with you.

2. Be creative. Bring plenty of colorful, tactile, fun items to school and invite the children to co-create their safe space either alone or in groups as meets their needs.

3. Think about bringing in light and space to reduce cognitive load, increase oxytocin, and facilitate a sense of belonging.

💡 It's not enough to invite children to the dance, we need to ask them out on the floor.

Reminder Oops!

When a teacher focuses negative attention on a child, a series of cascading effects result – all of which are counter-productive to the original intention.

The change in tone, body language, and cadence gets picked up by the child who becomes the center of negative attention and/or public shaming.

The child doesn't yet have white matter structures in place to process incoming sensory information. By denying the opportunity to focus attention on incoming sensory information, the teacher causes activation in the primal reactive loop involving the amygdala. This causes the learning moment to be about strengthening *that* reactive neural circuitry. The child did learn something – "I hate math, I hate this class, the teacher is mean… and I hate school."

What's Really Happening?

The resilient child will bounce back quickly and the negative attention diffuses. If the child is non-resilient, however, the damage can be much more permanent. Either way, the mere fact that the teacher isolated a child, changed tone, body language and cadence, will cause other sensitive children in the vicinity to lose attentive bonding and trust for that teacher.

"But, I wasn't even pointing towards those other kids – it was about that one specific misbehavior belonging to that one child." It doesn't work that way. All children feel the change – the tone, the cadence, and the body language. From their perspective, a vital trust has been destroyed.

A solid barrier has been raised between "me and the teacher." When the teacher works really hard to tear down that barrier with laughter, funny stories, even rewards, a double standard appears. On some days she seems okay, but beneath it all, she "picks" on some kids, the ones who are not able to focus. Hypervigilant children think, "One day soon, she will pick on me."

Morning Journey with Hippocampus

Leading children through visuospatial structures can help solidify memory. Consider this exercise:

Close your eyes. Think back to the first thing you remember this morning as you woke up. Did you wake because of an alarm, or does someone call you each morning? Recall what happened next. What did you do from the moment you woke up, to the moment you arrived in school?

Now choose one item – something that resonates because you really like doing it, or because you hate doing it. Draw a simple stick-figure sketch of it to capture how you feel about it. Turn to your partner, describe what you drew and explain why you chose this item. Then listen to your partner's description of the item that they chose. Finally, take the drawing home and place it under your pillow tonight as you sleep. In the morning, take out the drawing and as you engage in your day, note if there was anything out of sequence or something that you forgot to add.

How to Do it

1. Play this memory attention game in pairs, leading children through the exercise above. Give children 2 minutes with eyes closed to get into their memory processing neural circuits (particularly the visuospatial loop that connects episodic memories with spatial location and temporal accuracy).

2. Invite children to draw and relate to peers using whatever medium they choose for another 2 minutes. Sense of belonging is heightened in creative, fun activities.

3. Then, invite each pair to take turns sharing what they created and have fun as they articulate the "Me Here Now" of their lives.

💡 When children share emotional stories with partners, they grow closer to others.

Judgmental Cat & Mouse

Judgment ends up being a job description – it can feel like you're stuck trying to catch a child at something bad or wrong, rather than inspire them to learn.

This kind of thinking permeates many school systems. It causes an inherent "us vs. them" mindset for both students and educators. It feels like a constant "cat and mouse" game – except from the child's viewpoint, it's always going to end badly for the mouse at some point.

It is difficult to build connection and trust when you are constantly feeling judged (or judging). The idea that a teacher might hold a child hostage with something they really like to do, makes no sense in a world where learning is based on neuroscience.

What's Really Happening?

A mindset focused on judgment is seeking ways to trap the child. When a child makes a poor choice or a mistake, it is interpreted as wilful or defiant. How many times do we say, "learn from your mistakes"? But according to brain science, the child learns best when they have opportunities to play in the appropriate **fasciculi** (for instance in the phonological loop for language and articulation) and are *encouraged* to make mistakes in a safe, psychological environment that allows metacognitive and critical thinking to guide them.

Neurotransmitters play a central role in motivation and learning, activating the **midbrain dopamine system** that reacts to either appetitive or aversive stimuli. Research shows that humans actively seek rewards in their environment and are highly influenced by good experiences. Similarly, dopamine systems are highly influenced by aversive experiences that can deter motivation and learning. These negative experiences can resemble homework, detention, difficulties accessing mastery, and looking "dumb" in front of peers and family.

So, when you hear a child say, "I hate math," or "school sucks," know that these statements simply confirm that as educators, we have failed to create activities that release appropriate neurotransmitters (e.g. dopamine or oxytocin) in our learning spaces.

Be Curious!

What would happen if we could get to the bottom of the stressors that prevent a child from accessing their prefrontal cortex? What if we could find a way around issues like not getting enough sleep, or not having a safe place to do homework?

When teachers remain curious, inputs and outputs relating to the child change. Instead of perceiving the child as deliberately disruptive, put together a team of people who can help solve (or at least improve) a chaotic situation or eliminate a perceived barrier.

When you are curious and caring, solutions arise. A simple solution, in this case, might be to give the student an office desk for 30 minutes after school to finish projects, homework, or work with other children who also need a safe space to study.

There will be as many solutions as there are opportunities, and each one should align with needs that are specific to the child and the situation.

How to Do it

The curious teacher views the child from a place of potential. Ask yourself these questions to remain curious:

1. What is causing this learner to not be able to access their true potential?
2. How might I be able to reduce the amount or severity of stressors that are causing the child to react and disengage from their natural learning talent?
3. How can I work with other teachers to help make school more predictable and consistent and reduce making them feel overwhelmed in class?

💡 Dopamine works for teachers, too. When you stay childlike and curious, your classroom experience and relationships thrive.

Child needs Help

In every cohort of learners, you'll find children who are processing quickly, learning insatiably, and exceedingly happy to be challenged with new and difficult constructs.

At the same time, there will be several children who are not able to keep up with the rest of the learners. One reason is that they are missing key foundational constructs, which they failed to master in earlier learning environments. And in the middle, there are children who stay just below the radar, managing to get by with the bare minimum of effort.

These scenarios make life difficult for everyone. The fast processors get bored easily if the teacher adjusts the pace so that slower learners can catch up. The children who are having difficulty keeping up are easily overwhelmed, and are often pulled out of the classroom and consigned to paraeducators and remedial workers. And as the educator, you feel stuck between a rock and a hard place.

What's Really Happening?

When children are compared to each other through age or grade, these academic differences will inevitably show up. From a developmental standpoint, it makes very little sense to compare one child with another child just because they are the same age. Genetic and epigenetic factors can cause huge differences in outcomes, lived experience, and structures for taking-in and processing new information.

It may seem counterintuitive, yet experience verifies that teacher mindset, intentionality, and belief carry the day. A teacher who attempts to "push" children to improve their grades might accomplish the exact opposite outcome. Token economies and any form of reward or punishment will introduce barriers that prevent children from accessing their potential. It's not the teacher's fault, but it quickly becomes the teacher's problem. It is much more profitable to build strong relationships and help each child experience mastery.

Simplify Rubrics

Teachers who understand neural plasticity and the fact that a child's brain is entirely malleable, can make simple changes to their approach so that all learners can thrive.

It begins with vocabulary. Neural plasticity is real. While the child might have missed the opportunity to understand a concept in the past, there is always a new opportunity to grow a white matter structure for accessing information and processing it for deep understanding.

What kind of shift can the teacher make in order for the environment to change so the child will thrive? A simple first step is to simplify the **Rubric**. Focus only on one column – the exceeding column – and demonstrate that this child *can* exceed at any desired concept.

How to Do it

1. Begin with foundational material that is obviously causing the child to lag behind. Choose ONE concept and work to demonstrate how the child can learn and apply it.
2. Create a simple rubric with only ONE column that illustrates success.
3. Connect that ONE successful experience with similar opportunities for mastery.

💡 No child wants to lag behind. Mindset changes that favor all learners will lead to incredible growth in school and at home.

Time Out/Calm Down Corner

Certain patterns repeat in almost all learning spaces. Have you noticed how the same children get into amygdala hijack every day or week, regardless of whether they are studying for a test, learning math, or preparing for an amateur theatrical production?

The same kids are consigned to "Time Out" or "Calm Down Corner" solutions with an expectation that they will someday act like other children, which is judged to be more attuned to learning.

Sending children out of the crisis center and away from other children *does* solve one problem: it allows the teacher to focus their attention on the children who are "ready to learn."

Meanwhile, the child in the isolated spot is left to figure out how to return to the learning space alone.

What's Really Happening?

Regulation is not compliance. Compliance is not learning. Patterns do not confirm learning – they only signal the dysfunction of classrooms that are ill-prepared for high **ANS reactivity** brains.

All brains can and want to learn. So, when we notice that the same children are not able to learn day-to-day, we must question the suitability of the learning environment.

The learning environment includes the physical location and layout of the room, the body language and words of the teacher, the **Universal Design for Learning** plan that is uncovered for the children, and the mental models that all adults in the vicinity own and use with respect to the neuroscience of learning.

When we shift the environment, we are inviting ALL children to participate in their learning.

All I Need to Know...

It's as simple as this: all I need to know about any child is that they have a brain. All brains, while being unique and individual, work in roughly the same way.

All brains are hard-wired learning machines. So if the child fails to learn in your learning space, something is not right with the space. Make the change. Be curious... *Why would Mary learn here, but Maria is struggling? What can I change so that all my students are able to learn?* Behavior is communication. The child is telling you something about the space that prevents the brain from accessing information. The child might not be able to tell you directly, but they are certainly telling you.

Improving your learning environment is also simple; reduce the amount of cortisol by increasing predictability and certainty, increase the amount of oxytocin and dopamine. And have fun. Remember, if you are not having fun, you are not doing it right.

How to Do it

To improve your learning environment for all children, consider this:

1. Does the child *see* themselves as soon as they enter the learning space? Are there pictures, cultural artifacts, historical images, colors, toys, projects, and so on, that reflect each learner in your classroom?
2. How can you reduce the amount of ambient stimuli in the learning space, and instead invite the children to help decorate *their* room with you?
3. Experiment with vocabulary changes. For example, try: Magic Monday, Twosome Tuesday, Wobbly Wednesday, Brainy Thursday, and Fabulous Friday.

💡 When you make your classroom inviting for the high ANS Reactivity learner, you automatically make it inviting for all learners.

Neural Diversity

Every brain is unique. Yet for some reason, the educational landscape is divided into two camps; neuro-typical and neuro-diverse. My brain is different to yours, so which one of us is neuro-typical?

This two-dimensional way of thinking forces us to look deeper at some of the mainstays of neuroscience and learning that exist in every classroom. For instance, if teachers understand that neural plasticity is a tangible feature of learning, then there is room for all learners in their classrooms. All brains count.

As teachers and parents, it is not our job to fix children. Rather it is our *privilege* to adjust environments where possible so that all children can blossom and thrive. Thriving means that every individual has the opportunity to find what they are good at and lead a full and happy life full of purpose and friends.

What's Really Happening?

The first rule of teaching is "do no harm." When we label people based on a haphazard understanding of how neural plasticity works, we tend to "other" people who are different from us and, with these othering labels, do harm.

Some brains are more different than others. In schools, we encounter children who are born with neural networks that need more opportunities for creating and myelinating structures and circuits, so they can engage and live full life journeys. This same circuitry is already in place and more accessible to other children. Diversity is found in all learning communities including autism, ADHD, dysgraphia, dyscalculia, dyslexia. And yet, we all learn.

Neuroplasticity gives us methods and opportunities to nourish everyone's unique capacities and to find ways for every child to engage and contribute, to experience all the joys of life and to generate knowledge and skills.

Presume Competence

When we understand neurodiversity based on malleability, we are simply speaking about differences – not deficits. For instance, some children are non-speaking. That doesn't mean that they cannot communicate.

Expect that every child has a plan; every child has a dream. We treat all children with the same degree of respect.

Decide to expect high standards and amazing competence from children who are still building foundational structures and slowly myelinating these connections. It may take more time before they are able to show mastery, and you, as teacher, are willing to walk that journey to support them.

How to Do it

1. Take a deep breath. Before you discuss a child or speak to a child who has a different style of communication, ensure you are presuming competence in your approach.
2. Think about your message. Would you say these words to children who use verbal language to communicate?
3. Are you using their communication style to communicate with them? One way to be certain to connect to your students with different communication styles than your own is to use their form of communication with them.

💡 It is not our job to "fix" a child but to guide them, so they can achieve their own unique plans and dreams using the form of communication that is most valued and effective for the child.

Children Have No Energy

Even in a fun-filled happy classroom, there are times when children are stressed and show symptoms of reactive behavior indicative of anxiety, fear, and overwhelm. Teachers, too, can feel this way.

The automatic response to aversive behavior often results in changes to heart rate and other physiological responses that are described as that "icky feeling" in the belly.

Because of these physical responses to stress, children complain that they are feeling ill, need to go to the bathroom, or have pain in the tummy and ask to see the school nurse.

Either way, your class is disrupted and you lose a few children to the office or nurse's station.

What's Really Happening?

Environmental issues that are not present in the classroom may be inhibiting a child's progress in academics. Stressors spill over from home, the playground, the cafeteria, and even from inside the child's imagination. These stressors impact the child's immediate ability to focus and engage in classroom activities. This in turn hampers other children who are in the vicinity, causing them to get distracted and lose energy.

Dopamine is contagious. When the students are engaged and having fun, it is easy to maintain that energy. Similarly, **cortisol** is contagious. When a few children start to act out and disrupt, nearby children are impacted and may join in the disruptive behavior. What began as a single distraction can quickly escalate into a negative spiral that will significantly impede learning.

These negative spirals then prevent a child from accessing the higher-order processing capabilities of their rational and computational brain.

Belly Breathe

Negative downward spirals can easily be replaced with positive upwards spirals. The sooner you recognize the need and act to engage, the easier it will be to correct the flow of energy. By shifting the emphasis to a cognitive place, you are helping the child engage in a decentering exercise through **metacognition**. This only occurs with higher-order functioning in the **prefrontal cortex (PFC)**.

Decentering is a metacognitive awareness in which negative thoughts and feelings are seen as temporary transient mental events, rather than as aspects of self.

Practice during these metacognitive moments helps to cement decentering circuits in the child's thinking brain. This then allows for new experiences in abstract thinking, decision-making, and learning.

Deep breathing is critical for connection so that children feel the impact of ease. This breathing exercise is a whole brain, whole class, whole-body solution that delivers powerful positive energy as you build relations.

How to Do it

1. Ask students to stand comfortably. Every child should have enough room to stretch their arms out fully without interfering with any other person in the learning space.
2. Guide the students through belly breathing. Breathe in slowly, deeply widening the rib cage as they inhale.
3. Hold for two seconds, then exhale deeply by breathing out longer than you inhaled. Repeat at least 6 times. Very effective also with the Hoberman Sphere.

💡 A good breathing rate for this exercise is about six breaths per minute.

I'm Bored

It's easy to get upset with a child who complains that they are bored.

How could you possibly be bored? Look at all the toys you have, all those books, all those inventive games. You couldn't possibly be bored!

Unfortunately, this "When I was your age...." kind of thinking can lead to judgmental decisions and punishment.

We often get the same response with questions like "What did you do in school today?" Sometimes a child will tell you, especially if something novel or unusual occurred. However, the more frustrating responses are "Nothing," or "I don't know," or "School is boring."

To the unprepared, these can be very unsatisfactory answers and make parents or teachers wonder if there's something wrong with a child.

What's Really Happening?

Boredom can be good or it can be bad. It's important to listen to the child and acknowledge that they are seeking help. Boredom to the brain can feel the same as stress, as it lights up similar areas in the brain.

Typically, if the subject matter is focused on content, as opposed to being child-centric, then the child may feel unengaged. When the material doesn't relate to them, they struggle to focus on information about something else, over there, at some other time. This is the exact opposite to how the brain works with **Me Here Now**!

When is boredom good? The brain has a default mode where quiet is normal. Children are usually not aware of this mode. It is often associated with amazing creativity and innovative thinking. Just knowing about its existence helps reframe boredom for the child.

Brilliant Bored Brain

Be curious! What could cause this child to be feeling bored right now? Could it be that they are afraid, feeling left out, feeling not able, or the material had no meaning for them?

Or, could it be that they already know this material well? Have you ever heard, "We did this last year and I don't want to waste time with it again. Just because the rest of the class is behind me, doesn't mean that I should be kept back"? This is an easy solution when a jigsaw approach is used. Children with different abilities and experiences are able to assist other children who are discovering this material for the first time.

Universal Design for Learning (UDL) methods allow for flexibility and equity in classrooms. All children can involve themselves at the level they find themselves. As an educator, you look for suitable access points so the child can feel included at a level that works. Think classroom environment - universally designed for all.

How to Do it

1. Prepare lessons with multiple access points so that all children are able to feel **Me Here Now** in every class.
2. Universal design environments will involve hard work at building relationships, not only with the child, but with the four consistent caring adults that greenhouse them.
3. Each child will find opportunities to find their voice and engage in co-creating each lesson by sticking to the model of the 3 R's: Reflect, Revised Thinking and Report Out.

💡 Boredom can be put to good use through discerning curiosity.

Child-Centric?

Every school claims to be child-centric. Yet when we look closer, it is easy to see that while the school system *is* really trying to do the best thing for the child, the program is entirely and consistently content-centric, or behavior-centric.

These are not bad goals per se – but they certainly are not child-centric.

So what is a true child-centric approach?

What's Really Happening?

The true genius of the teacher is made visible when we focus on the child's appetite rather than their aptitude. Consistent with a neural knowledge that "affect" precedes "effect", the child is more important than the content.

A child-centric approach focuses on a personalized program that does two things:

1. The child is never compared with or against other children (regardless of age).
2. Content builds naturally as a child's neural, developmental, and social-emotional knowledge progresses.

In other words, educators use content to architect the child's brain, not the other way around (filling up the brain with content).

Methods and interventions do not always help. Some well-meaning interventions will have memorable acronyms that promise to deliver positive outcomes and good behavior. Yet in spite of the aspirational nomenclature, they fail to deliver anything that equates to classroom success or behavior that equates to better engagement and learning. Many teachers equate methods that cause compliance as desirable teaching practice.

It quickly becomes clear that compliance is neither synonymous with learning, nor with education.

Appetite Over Aptitude

Most teachers enter the profession because they were impressed and inspired by a particular teacher and want to re-create a best-outcome social impact for next generation scholars.

Conversely, some teachers were so horrified by a most-hated, terrible teacher, that they want to reverse a worst-outcome social impact and save new generations of children from the suffering that they so vividly recall. This doesn't mean that teachers are better at their profession merely because of these aspirational ideals.

All children need the support of **FOUR Consistent Caring** adults. That might seem like an easy thing to achieve. In some cultures it's not a problem. It takes a little effort to refresh a frame – a mental model – that allows this child-centric approach to flourish. Helping children find these adults is key to true child-centric learning.

How to Do it

1. Help a child identify their 4 consistent caring adults. Every child's brain is hardwired to make relationships with healthy emotional bonds.
2. Be patient. This isn't always easy. It takes planning, vision and dedication; it takes time, organization and cooperation. And yes, it can be the most important support that any child can get.
3. Look in new places. For some children, these adults may be hard to find. The soccer coach, the cafeteria attendant who high-fives the child every day, the grandma who shows up to watch volleyball games – these are life changing helpers.

💡 Every child could be one caring adult away from being a fabulous success story!

Section III: Reason

Brain is not destiny. One can't learn Algebra when being chased by a tiger. Tiger Schmiger...there are no tigers!

– Kieran O'Mahony, PhD, FRGS

Kids These Days

We are very familiar with disruptive kids. Some of us might even have been considered "disruptive" when we were in school. All teachers are challenged by a few children who either don't have the will to learn, the attention span, or the desire to try. "Oppositional" even "aggressive" is how some teachers see these learners. They are not compliant and are therefore difficult to manage and slow to learn.

- A neural lens changes all that
- Teachers think about and are able to change classroom environments so that children feel they can be successful
- A reasoning child is a related-to child and a child who is able to learn
- A child's experience improves; teacher's experience improves and classrooms become positive contagious learning spaces for fun and success

The notion of "us versus them" mentality goes away. Teachers co-create with their students and together they build teams of collaborating and fun-loving learners that know success. The old learned practices are adjusted so that "environment" is primary, and children's access to their potential is the outcome. Teachers learn to navigate system-wide district policies that often pose threats to positive learning experiences. And especially, teachers avoid the urge to fall back into discipline methods that they experienced themselves when they were in school, or learned from their parents at home.

Teachers can easily avoid myelinating a mindset of "kids these days" – that these children are simply not able or willing. It's a mistake to fall into the trap of thinking that compliance is a silver bullet. The truth is, when it comes to teaching, there are very few silver bullets. And more importantly, compliance is *not* synonymous with learning. A neural lens in the classroom is the best way to encounter great learning.

Compliance is NOT Learning
All children have brains that are hardwired to learn. In fact, if we did nothing, children would continue to learn the same way they did as infants – vacuuming up all kinds of meaningful information that helped them make sense of their newly emerging world.

Many parents lament the loss of their ultra-curious, precocious child that became "compliant" as soon as they entered school. School seemed to become synonymous with loss of autonomy, loss of fun, loss of freedoms. All replaced with a whole lot of adherence to rules and traditions that didn't have any particular meaning to the child.

Today, we are interested in personalized learning: creating experiences that allow children to follow their **Appetite**, knowing that it will also activate their **Aptitude**. From the brain's point of view, if it has some relevance to ME, HERE, NOW, then I'm all in. But if it is about something else, some other place, or some other time, I can't get excited about it.

The particular genius of teachers is their genuine capacity to connect relevant new information to any child so that the ME, HERE, NOW activates **Prior Knowledge** and connects with new information. But classrooms are not typically built to accommodate learning. Depending on the electronic system that has been installed, the child might experience damaging "reminders", visible and public "shaming", and progressive, punitive practices that can be both harmful and long-lasting. Competition only works for some kids.

Competitive methods include whiteboard accessories that can quickly highlight how every child is progressing in a class – positive and negative visualizations with color codes and statuses that help label, stratify, and isolate. Many school systems view children through a lens of behavior.

- Compliant
- At Risk
- High Risk

Through a Neural Lens - behavior is simply communication. When we look for the neural substrate that explains behavior, we are able to solve behavior, and therefore solve children. In Section Three - Reason, we introduce a brain-based pedagogic model that guides a class of learners into self-efficacy and critical thinking. The elements of this model are explained: Disequilibrium, Challenge, Initial Thoughts, Multiple Perspectives, carefully scaffolded 3 Cognitive R's, and Long-Term Potentiation.

Persistence of Misconceptions

Learners, no matter how old or experienced, do not show up at the knowledge table with a clean slate. There is no *Tabula Rasa*. We all come to the table with mental models because we have *de facto* made sense of our world.

It is easy to recognize that, left to our own devices, sense-making can be flawed – misconceptions, preconceptions, and received opinion. There is always room for learning.

It turns out that the **persistence of misconceptions** is universal and manifest. Even if the mouth says, *"I get it … I understand,"* people invariably **revert to default** by refusing to let go of earlier convictions, and by continuing to embrace earlier misconceptions.

For this reason, a moment of disequilibrium is ideal for upturning pre-determined thinking so that new meaning can replace previous thinking.

Conceptual change is about letting go and assimilating. *"I used to think about it this way, but with new information I can see it another way."*

When a child experiences prior knowledge being replaced by new knowledge, the mental "journey" is made visible. It's actually *my* journey through knowledge and it is deeply meaningful to, and for, me.

What's Really Happening?

The **reticular activating system (RAS)** is designed to confirm our beliefs. If we have already made sense of the world so that we are satisfied and know closure, then it is going to take something momentous to shift our thinking. A carefully crafted moment of disequilibrium is the perfect antidote to fixedness and old ill-informed mental models.

Disequilibrium

Attentional arousal through disequilibrium is very powerful and long-lasting. But long-lasting (unlike persistent) is only good when it describes the true state of things. For instance, the old adage that "practice makes perfect" only works if the practice is perfect. Practice makes permanent!

This is why mediated practice by an expert, like a teacher or a parent, makes all the difference. We must be intentional about practice when mental models coincide with meaning-making. Disequilibrium is not the same as putting big red X's or wrong marks on a child's math quiz. Sure, it will get the attention of the learner, but at least 50% of the time, it will convince the learner that they are never going to be any good at math. This outcome is not what the very thoughtful teacher intends with those long hours of correcting and assigning children's scores.

How to Do it

1. Give feedback immediately, meaningfully, and compassionately. Do not make feedback punitive. You don't always have to point out every mistake to correct a misconception.
2. Be on the lookout for fun, entertaining and challenging videos to incorporate in the classroom.
3. Ensure that your disequilibrium connects with a big question. What can you ask to drive the message home? Remember to bring it back to **Me Here Now.** All children have a plan, a purpose. Connect your disequilibrium with their plan.

💡 Disequilibrium will set the tone for eager, fun learning and long-lasting memories. It causes the learner to lean in and get curious about what's going to happen next.

I'm Lost

Sometimes, no matter how much you encourage a child, they just don't progress.

In a high-stakes competitive learning environment, at least 50% of children will not be able to find mastery on any given day. But in order to survive academically, they need to have successful mastery episodes every hour.

Given the tendency of the survival brain to automatically go negative 80% of the time, these children find themselves in a perpetual "red zone" or survival mode.

Hyper-vigilance, learned helplessness, and negative self-talk is reinforced by their **reticular activating systems (RAS).** This works against even your best attempts at motivating these children.

What's Really Happening?

When the RAS overrides positive reinforcement, use intentionality. Intentionality in mastery requires a deliberate effort to help the child see their starting place and a finishing place. The co-created learning events that you enable will help the child easily understand the difference and reach mastery.

A moment of intentional quiet allows the brain to collect itself and focus on the task at hand in a psychologically safe environment. No one sees the child's output, so there is no judgment, grades, or comments. The child is able to treat this as a starting place where it is safe to make a prediction about the work in hand. This higher-order thinking skill can only happen in the executive frontal lobe where academic output is readily achieved.

At first, this mastery monitor will be good practice and over time, it will become a powerful myelinated neuronal tract that facilitates critical and original thinking.

Mastering Mastery

An exercise in **Initial Thoughts** can help override the RAS and put a child on the path to mastery. Establish a classroom norm that when a new topic is introduced there is a one-minute, single-task moment to breathe, process information, and collect meaningful thoughts.

In the beginning, many children might not be able to collect their initial thoughts. They may experience a stressful threat response that causes negative self-evaluation, social evaluative threat, and negative self-spiral into freeze, fight, flight, or fawn.

Make it clear that it is okay to write "IDK." It doesn't really matter what the child writes, as long as they get to experience an adult inviting them to calm their mind, focus their thinking, and make a prediction about their own knowledge in a safe psychological space. After a few iterations, the child will replace IDK with verbiage that is meaningful to their ability to grasp new information. This is the essential building block to original thinking.

How to Do it

1. Invite the child to "single-task" for one minute in relation to the challenge (content material), that is your big idea for the lesson. Most children will need to be shown what "single-task" means. Treat the construct as a verb; single-tasking is spending one minute in silence to think, collect thoughts, write a few notes, or scribble.

2. Make it clear that it is the child's minute of quiet; no one will ever ask to see what they wrote or share it without permission.

3. Intentionally connect the **Reflect** exercise and three scaffolding questions disclosed earlier to **Initial Thoughts,** so that it is clear to the child where mastery lives.

💡 Initial Thoughts are to Mastery, as pencils are to writing; it's a path to mastery.

Right or Wrong

In the traditional two-dimensional classroom, children are taught to seek out the right answer and avoid a wrong answer.

When the sensitive learner gets something wrong instead of right, they are likely to be reminded by their **RAS** that, "Yes, you know you are not able to do this hard work, so why try?" One of the myelinated outcomes might be that the child's **Mindset** becomes even more **Fixed** with regard to their own capacity to learn.

What's Really Happening?

When we are more interested in architecting a child's brain so that they co-construct white matter circuitry to enable critical thinking, problem-solving, and celebrating their intelligent contribution to life, then we are *not* interested in a two-dimensional way of looking at school.

When the same sensitive learner gets an opportunity to come up with ideas based on three simple and persistent scaffolding questions, they are connecting important neuronal structures (white matter tracts) from the back of the head to the front, and from one hemisphere to the other. This practice strengthens neurons that fire together so that they wire together and through **Plasticity** increase the child's capacity as a learner.

By offering differing **Perspectives** related to a real-world challenge, children have an opportunity to **Reflect** on, and then **Revise** their thinking about a solution that they can understand.

Multiple Perspectives

Multiple perspectives capture attention and engage a learner's brain in the pursuit of a solution to a meaningful challenge. There are no right or wrong answers, simply different interpretations based on the perspectives from different regions of the brain (auditory, visual, tactile, and others).

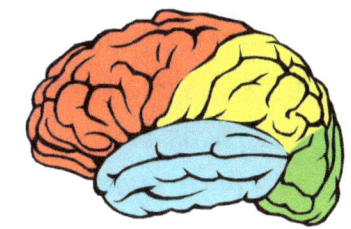

Intentionality about including the cerebellum causes the child to process in all lobes, while also connecting with movement and balance. Reading, writing, and auditory connections are easy to highlight with video and note-taking interactive planning. Sense of smell, touch, and feel are also easy to include with a little curious problem-solving.

A combination of cognitive and small-motor skills enhances a child's sense of belonging, understanding of mastery, and self-efficacy toward a meaningful purpose.

How to Do it

1. Curate material that advances a child's capacity to use their whole brain. Begin with a challenge that is personalized to each child in the cohort. Find a way to connect the lesson with each child's **Me Here Now**. This is the particular genius of the cognitive teacher.

2. The challenge is not seeking a right or wrong answer, but practicing focused engagement where all children generate ideas and contribute to a solution.

3. As you prepare your multiple perspectives, think about how the cerebellum and each lobe of the brain can be involved in the process; occipital, temporal, parietal, and frontal.

💡 Whole-brain, child-centric teaching allows every child to engage in the challenge and outcome.

Inert Scraps Take Up Space

When you ask the question, "What did you learn in school today?" and a child responds with "nothing..." it is not because they didn't learn anything or are upset with you. If they understood the construct of **Active Avoidance**, they might say *"I learned a disconnected scrap of inert knowledge because I was **actively avoiding** detention and wanted to attain C+ in yet another meaningless quiz."*

Each second, your brain is bombarded with more than 11 million bits of information. There are roughly 30,000 seconds in a child's school day. That's something like 330 *billion* bits of information bombarding the child's brain every school day.

Because of school, our brains are chock-a-block with scraps of information that are not connected to anything meaningful (like extraneous lines of poetry you were forced to memorize as a child, lines that still pop up at the most inopportune moments).

What's Really Happening?

Scraps of information are not the same as learning. These scraps are essentially taking up space that could be used for doing something that could be considered more productive. They feel disconnected because they are not speaking to **Me Here Now.**

With so much information coming into our brains each second, it's lucky we have the RAS to act as a filter. So how does the RAS know what to allow into conscious experience and what to ignore or keep out? RAS is carefully trained to allow in information that is connected, that resonates with what you know is true; information that yells "Me Here Now!"

Reflect Collects Your Thoughts

"Reflect" is an active brain-based activity that is carefully scaffolded to optimize working memory and critical thinking.

For the Reflect exercise, the child works alone with their current thoughts, predictions, and prior knowledge. The scaffolding questions curate the thought process so that meaningful connections are made to recent "multiple perspectives" and aligned back to the lesson's Big Idea.

Three scaffolding questions are strategically ordered so that the initial question lays the groundwork for question two and so on.

Each question is prioritized to affect the neural substrates of behavior. The question about surprise is designed to free the learner from any negative feedback that might cause amygdala hijack. Question two invites the learner to see their thinking shift. Question three invites vulnerability – a key element of asking for help.

How to Do it

1. Start Reflect, a 2-minute hands-on activity where the learner is directed to answer three scaffolding questions that capture their thinking: What was surprising? What did you already know but now see differently? What do you still need help with?

2. As the facilitator, observe the 2-minute silence with no cross-talk, no overtalk, no editorializing or explanation. This is the learner's time for thinking.

3. Two minutes is easily enough time for a child to get thinking down on paper or a tech device so that they are armed with a personalized reflection for Revised Thinking.

💡 Reflect helps the child capture what is in their working memory and make it applicable to Me Here Now.

Rote Memorization is Real

Cramming for a test and use of repetition for recall during examinations, typically results in the following outcomes:

- Students are studying just to get a good score.
- Students learn to regurgitate information, not deeply understand it.
- Once the test is over, children forget most of the information (**Ebbinghaus Forgetting Curve**).
- Cramming and regurgitating does not help problem-solving.
- Students fail to realize the real-life application of the information they are regurgitating.

Twenty-first-century learners are ideally preparing for a future that is not even possible to envision.

Metacognitive practices and critical and original thinking are more appropriate for **Preparation for Future Learning (PFL).**

What's Really Happening?

There *is* a place for rote memorization in schools. It makes good sense to encode nursery rhymes, alphabet, multiplication tables, and other easy and fun elements of learning that will remain as pillars of computation throughout one's life. Fun and easy usually means that music, rhythm, and games are used to help with the encoding.

However, rote memorization for automaticity of use later differs from rote memorization of inert items of information that lack that significance. For instance, it makes no sense to recall that in 1922 Shackleton died in South Georgia, if the child fails to understand the significance of polar exploration or man's capacity for endurance.

Rote memory techniques, like using flashcards and quizzes, are common practices in order to pass a test or get a good grade. The problem is, this kind of learning has long-lasting implications that might not be in the best interest of the learner.

Revised Thinking is Magic

Not all children like to work in small groups. However, when a child's opinion matters, then they are able to generate new ideas. And when other children learn from their ideas, they quickly become embroiled in an intrinsically-motivated learning activity.

Once again, it's a matter of **Me Here Now**. The brain can handle the stress of shyness, anxiety, and fear of public speaking, when the child is the center of the action (generating, contributing, and teaching). In fact, these same children learn a great deal when given the opportunity to compare and contrast their ideas with their peers in a psychologically safe environment, especially when they are part of the co-creation of that safe environment.

Revised Thinking is where the "magic" is reported by learners. They become energized and enter a flow state when they find that their voice matters, their ideas are good and their peers are willing to share and listen.

How to Do it

1. Create small groups of 6 or 7, where there are enough individuals to solve problems, but each child still has a voice in the group.
2. Each group decides 4 roles to manage time and inquiry: **Facilitator, Time Keeper, Scribe,** and **Report Out.**
3. Invite each participant to share information that was captured in **Reflect** earlier: What was surprising? What did you know, but now see differently? And what do you still need help with?

> 💡 Revised Thinking is where individuals find their voice and learn to thrive.

Limping Alone in Tall Grass

No one wants to limp alone in dangerous geography. This applies to the geography of the mind as well. It can be scary to find yourself alone in a hostile environment with ideas, words, and thoughts that let you down.

How many times have you experienced what so many children do in the classroom: you know the answer or a very good solution, but the moment you open your mouth, it's gone? Something else comes out, or you lose your train of thought entirely.

At a time when a child needs support most, many teachers don't give them the time to gather their thoughts or work their way back to their answer or idea. They are left alone in the geography of their mind. Trust is broken and they resolve never to put themselves in that place of discomfort again.

What's Really Happening?

This place of discomfort is exactly what is needed for each learner to rewire their brain and make new and powerful connections to new information and understanding. The brain grows by experiencing an authentic struggle to attain a sense of proficiency and skill in a particular arena of knowledge.

Sadly, this only works when there is a safe psychological learning space where the individual is encouraged to take risks, step outside their comfort zone, be ready to make mistakes and regroup with a new effort, if necessary.

The good news is that the brain is always building, myelinating, and strengthening neuronal circuits that relate to experiences in the learning space. The bad news is that the brain is always building, myelinating, and strengthening neuronal circuits that relate to experiences in the learning space. If the experiences are not ideal, the brain will strengthen circuits that prohibit the learner from excelling in the very field of experience that is desired by the lesson and the teacher. The genius of teachers is that they can guide the brain to good news.

Middle of the Herd Report Out

WE is the most important realization in the strategy of **Report Out**. This is a carefully sculpted learning exercise that encapsulates a single lesson, a series of lessons in a theme, or an entire section of new content material relevant to a fresh module of learning by using the power of a group.

Each child's voice is in the WE. It is not necessary to stand in front of peers, to report to the larger group, and yet the child is able to feel the representation of generated ideas, contributions, and salient questions.

The WE connection to **Me Here Now** is significant, evocative, and long-lasting. Every child is included. All voices matter. Equity, inclusivity, and equality of opportunity are not only evident, but highly tangible.

When a solid cohort of co-creating peers support each other, safety is apparent, learning is evident, and fear of the success of others dissipates.

How to Do it

1. Start by asking each group to choose a name that best describes who they are and how they came to be in this **Report Out** position. "WE are the…"

2. All members of each small workgroup converge together for the **Report Out** activity so that everyone knows with clarity that their voice is included and important.

3. The spokesperson begins with the word "We" and includes the remainder of the guiding questions in the sentence: "WE were surprised by… WE knew this… now WE … WE need help…"

> 💡 Report Out allows every child to access their agency in a safe environment, so big ideas can flourish.

No We Didn't...

At some point in a teacher's journey, a child will state with complete (and emotional) conviction, "We *never* learned that!" referring to material that the teacher covered in the recent past (perhaps as recent as the day before).

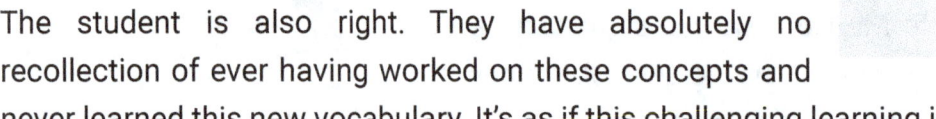

The teacher is right. Indeed, they had spent at least 20 minutes working through the concepts and practicing a new vocabulary associated with that particular topic. As far as she is concerned, the material was taught and the children should be able to recall it.

The student is also right. They have absolutely no recollection of ever having worked on these concepts and never learned this new vocabulary. It's as if this challenging learning is a new and devious trick that the teacher is playing on them. It never happened.

What's Really Happening?

Learning is not the same as remembering. From the brain's point of view, learning happens when neurons *fire together* and subsequently *wire together*. If there is sufficient **cognitive rehearsal**, **white matter structures** associated with the new construct are able to **myelinate** and **consolidate**.

Learning consolidation takes place during sleep. If the student doesn't get solid sleep (usually eight hours, uninterrupted), the tiny **dendritic spines** that are associated with the memory of the lesson can disappear. A physical change occurs during sleep, which will either **consolidate** the learning or eliminate the memory of having had the learning.

Perhaps the child did have a solid eight hours of sleep and is still claiming that they never learned this new material. Well, memory is flawed. And learning is as haphazard as flawed memory. It comes down to **cognitive rehearsal**. Just because the teacher spoke about this new material and used the whiteboard to illustrate some new vocabulary, does not guarantee that the student was able to access or process this new material.

Long Lasting Connections

If the child learns something, it's because of the brain. If they don't learn, it's also because of the brain. So, brain-based teaching includes notions of **whole-brain** and **child-centric** teaching.

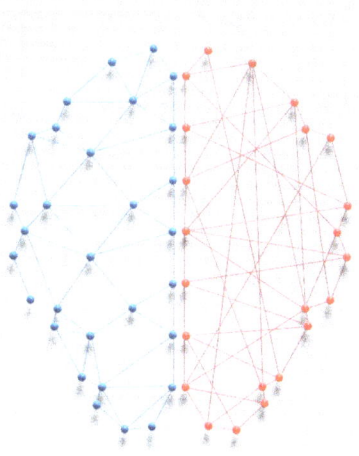

When the teacher has not only the vocabulary but also the associated mental models that enable and enhance learning, then the child's capacity will be lifelong and deep.

Try this exercise to grow long-lasting connections:

- New challenging information is personalized to the learner in a fun and non-threatening way.
- Child receives several opportunities for cognitive rehearsal using the cerebellum and four lobes.
- Child has an opportunity to reflect on and then revise their thinking about the new information.
- Child has the opportunity to practice agency with this new knowledge and associated vocabulary.

How to Do it

1. Be intentional about making space and time for children to process at the end of a lesson. Invite each child to draw a picture or write a word that captures their thinking.
2. Provide a space (online or physical) where their picture or word is stored until the next time you meet to continue the learning.
3. Start the next lesson by choosing one of the items and inviting its owner to share why they chose this item and what it means to them.

💡 Synapse is the currency of learning.

Tiered Systems

What if the "Compliant - At Risk - High Risk" tiered system didn't have to be used to describe a child's brain?

When a parent hands over their amazing child to the capable hands of educators, they expect that we do our best with their precious cargo. And in return, we label and stratify their children from day one. This is wrong, wholly wrong!

Somehow we have normalized this 3-tier system that highlights compliant children – children that are easy to teach. Next, we highlight a number of "at risk" kids who, on particular days, slip into unmanageability that requires increased attention from the teacher. And finally, there are the "high-risk" children who are often oppositional, disruptive, and ill-prepared to contribute to any learning space. The kids are familiar with trips to the principal's office. They're in and out of school detentions.

What's Really Happening?

Traditional methods work for some children. But in most cases, teachers, parents, and children all express frustration at how painful and ineffective these interventions are. When we approach the challenge from a neural standpoint, we discover more effective (and very much less painful) ways to interpret the student who is falling behind and provide different ways to intervene by changing the learning environment to deliver desired results.

Viewed through a neural lens, these children are missing requisite white matter structures that other children seem to have in spades. Because of environmental or genetic factors, the "compliant" children are wired with super-highways for good processing power that promotes engagement, attachment, friendships, and more – all skills and traits that enhance success in early learning. So, how can we help all children create this wiring in their brains?

A Child's Brain

Every child is hardwired to excel at math and to be an avid reader. It is built into our nature as *sapiens*. So why might a child struggle in a particular subject? Perhaps, if we stopped comparing one child against another just because they share the same age, we might at least begin to think about the neural substrate that is a causal link to innate ability in reading and/or math.

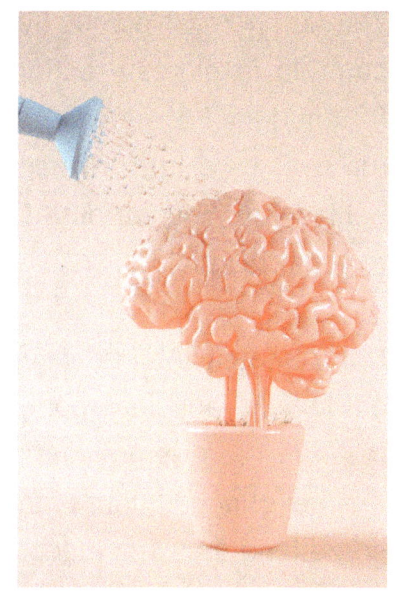

The best way for children to build the structures that will give them a proficiency in math and reading, is to play and make *fun mistakes* in the phonological loop and in the visuospatial sketchpad.

This is how they acquire myelinated white matter structures that allow them to excel in learning. It is not our job to punish them when they have not YET built these critical structures. Rather, it is our job to facilitate a learning environment that allows children to build these white matter cognitive circuits!

How to Do it

1. Use the phonological loop to activate the fun of discovery. Exploratory word games are great because they accomplish two things: they build myelinated white matter structures in Broca's and Wernicke's area and foster a love of language.

2. Use the visuospatial sketchpad to activate play. This accomplishes two more things: builds myelinated white matter structures that connect the temporal, parietal and prefrontal cortex.

3. Foster a safe, psychological, non-competitive, inclusive learning space that invites all children to generate ideas and contribute through autonomy, mastery and purpose.

💡 Avoid competition, comparison, and punishment. Fun mistakes help all children thrive.

Autonomic Nervous System Reactivity

The Autonomic Nervous System is the matrix of nerves that controls involuntary actions – actions that don't require forethought. For instance, you don't think, "I am going to get run over by a truck," when you hear the squeal of brakes behind you. You jolt out of harm's way involuntarily, thanks to your amygdala.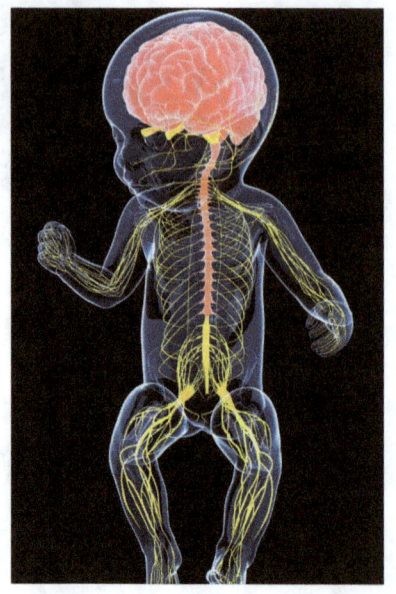

Unfortunately, ANS reactivity is not so protective in social context. In your classroom, a child's amygdala might decide that the room is not "safe" anymore. Maybe because the teacher changed their tone of voice when another child did something that was inappropriate. The child saw how they reacted to that behavior and now they are afraid that the teacher is going to do the same thing to them. Their amygdala shuts down access to their rational, thinking brain and learning stops.

What's Really Happening?

When this happens, it's not your fault or the child's fault. It's just how the brain is. Knowing your own ANS reactivity score can help you see how you fit on a continuum between sensitivity and resilience. The degree to which you can bounce back after a personal setback when someone presses your buttons, or how you interact in life is a good indicator of where you reside on this scale. For instance, I am an "in-betweener," – I am easily hurt by someone's unkind words. Yet, recognizing my sensitivity, I can take a deep breath and regulate myself.

The journey from sensitivity to resilience is a practice I find easy because I understand what's happening. However, children do not yet know what sensitivity or resilience means. So, their lives can be entirely reactive in amygdala hijack 100% of the time. These children seem difficult to teach because they interpret body language, words, and environments as unsafe and threatening. But, children who have learned the vocabulary and mental models about the continuum between resilience and sensitivity, are able to co-regulate with you first and then, self-regulate.

School-Friendly Genetics

The child's characteristics you see in your classroom are the result of the interaction between their genotype and the environment. So, the type of classroom you create will cause the child to adopt the characteristics you observe.

Psychological safety is predicted by a child's **ANS reactivity.** Some children are born with "short-short" expressions of the Serotonin Transporter Gene. It's not their fault that they do not get as much serotonin as other children.

In your classroom, it is possible to infuse serotonin by using words, body language, and intrinsic motivation so that every child experiences autonomy, mastery and purpose in their daily activities.

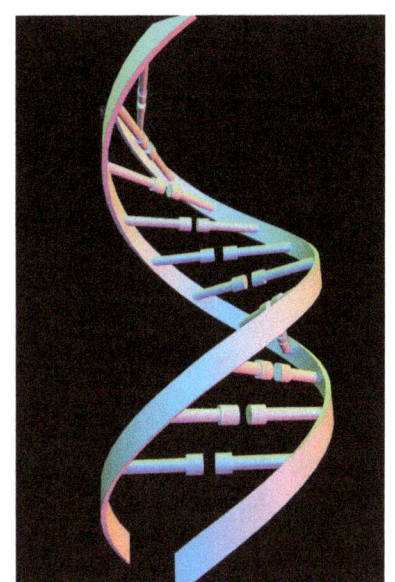

How to Do it

1. Put yourself in your students' shoes. As a child walks into your classroom, would they see themselves in a safe happy fun place? Take note of any experiences that may cause an amygdala hijack. How can you minimize these?

2. Now consider: How could you create an inclusive, fun place that screams "You are valued," "I love learning with you," and "school is fun for all of us"?

3. Think beyond the classroom. Social context occurs in hallways, cafeterias, playgrounds, or anywhere a child may fear a social evaluative threat, engagement, or competition.

💡 Social context is to genes, as sleep is to bones. We need it to be safe to grow.

Negative Priming

You may notice students who say these words (and they end up coming true):

I'm always late.
I'm no good at (whatever subject).
School sucks, my life sucks.

This is the **Reticular Activating System (RAS)** at work. If we knew that we had the RAS, we would approach many things in our lives very differently. In particular, we educators would show up differently in our learning spaces.

It's quite amazing what a small clump of neurons that live on the brain stem can cause to occur and affect our life journey. Basically, the RAS's job is to confirm your beliefs all day long. If I *believe* I am no good at math, my RAS will interpret those corrective red marks on my homework as proof. RAS will confirm your beliefs. That's its job.

What's Really Happening?

Every second, your brain receives roughly 11 million bits of information from internal organs in the body and external stimulants in your environment. The brain cannot process all that information in conscious time and space – it does this unconsciously thanks to the RAS.

The RAS decides what the brain should focus on, by bringing only some items to your conscious awareness. If you decide to purchase a blue Tesla, you will find blue Teslas showing up as if by magic. No magic; just science. You programmed your RAS to look for blue Teslas. In the same way, you program your students' RAS to love learning or fear learning. Especially for your sensitive orchid children, it is easy to convince their RAS that school sucks and that they are not as capable as their peers. Once their beliefs are solidified, it's hard to go back. Even if you say, "You are good enough to succeed," their RAS will override your words and confirm their innermost feeling that they are not good enough.

RAS-ify Your Children

The good news is we own our RAS. We can change it – and help children change theirs.

It comes down to words. Words have power. Some words carry weight that defines them as negative with downward spiraling momentum. Consider the first three words versus the last three words of this list:

Blame, Disappoint, Punish / Trust, Satisfied, Harmony.

Knowledge about their RAS can empower children; they need not be victims to its unseen outcomes. It's important to help children understand their RAS, and use it to foster learning and achievement.

How to Do it

1. Try affirmations. Co-created affirmations with evidence are fail-proof. For example, "I know I am good at math, because I have already learned to….." (insert a skill the child has achieved).
2. The RAS is susceptible to social context. Ensure that the environment you create in your learning space is safe and welcoming.
3. Avoid reward systems. It seems counter intuitive, but think about the negative impact that creeps into your learning space when children see others getting a reward that they hoped to get.
4. Experiences are contagious. When something goes right, everyone feels it. When something goes wrong, everyone feels it also. Feelings both positive and negative are contagious. Maintain an upbeat positive mood about life, peers, work, food, games, and yourself. Children will learn from this feeling.

💡 Children learn when they are able; social context is crucial to enable that learning.

If...Then Mistake

If you behave like everyone else, then you will earn a gold star. If you do not, then you will not be allowed to play baseball with the other kids at recess.

It's easy for educators to link behavior to a reward or a punishment. We grew up in the mindset that good equates to reward, bad equates to punishment. What we didn't know back then, was the negative limiting effect that both rewards and punishments delivered to the learning brain.

The learning brain thrives on intrinsic motivation. This means a little autonomy, lots of mastery, and a connection to purpose. The enduring take-away idea is that if there is even a tiny amount of cognitive load involved in a task, rewards produce the exact opposite outcome to what was expected. The science is clear: intrinsic methods beat extrinsic for all cognitive tasks.

What's Really Happening?

In a two-dimensional behaviorist world, (right or wrong, good or bad, sit quiet, do not talk), the child is expected to adjust behavior in line with teacher expectations. The problem is 21st century children do not live in a two-dimensional world.

And behavior is simply communication. If the child shows you that they cannot focus or pay attention, it doesn't mean that the child is deliberately misbehaving. It is a lot more likely that the "misbehaving" child is telling you that something is lacking in the environment that will enable them to grow the white matter structures needed for focus.

Today's child loves to learn about their brain and how to architect it so that it can generate ideas, contribute through critical thinking. If you practice activities that *grow* these white matter tracts, instead of relying on rewards and punishment, the child (and all others in the class) will learn to pay attention and become focused at will.

No Strings Attached

School is the most fun a child could experience *when* we plan school with fun. The only way that children would lose trust, feel left out, feel pushed out, or not included, is when teachers misuse or exploit the fun desires associated with learning and socializing, to isolate and punish.

Fun is easy to plan and neural structures are easy to grow. Children grow them every day. It is our job as parents and teachers to support this. Yet sadly, many of the structures that children grow in a behaviorist world tend to be structures that drive defense mechanisms, learned helplessness, and survival freeze, fight, flight, and fawn capabilities.

"No Strings Attached" is a mindset shift. With this practice, there are no "strings" – rewards or punishments – attached to behavior so that the learning environment is predictable, consistent, and kind for all children. This exercise helps the 50% of children who are less resilient and generally more hypervigilant, grow the structures they need to thrive. All children should experience joy, not just the ones that are compliant.

How to Do it

1. Make surprises and other fun and novel activities that happen in the classroom every day, as part of your teaching strategy.
2. Make efforts to co-create the learning space by inviting all the children to not only generate ideas, but especially to implement and "own" those ideas.
3. When children know that you are fair and non-judgmental, all the children can learn.

💡 There is no need to link behavior to rewards or punishments; all children want to learn.

Cortisol Effect

At the right time and in the right dosage, cortisol is a lifesaver. Crucially, at the wrong time and in a severe and persistent dosage, cortisol is a harbinger of disease and death. The child who is afraid of math, who is convinced that they are no good at math, whose RAS confirms this fact every day, will experience a cortisol surge as soon as someone says, "Get out your math book and let's do some exciting new math."

This is not the effect that a teacher wants. In fact, it is not the effect that anyone wants. Yet it happens in classrooms everyday all across the country. Look at the math results from this year's (or any year's) Nation's Report Card by NAEP (National Association for Education Performance). This is quite a depressing report, and has been for fifty years.

What's Really Happening?

Cortisol is released in response to a stressor. It prepares the body for a fight-or-flight response. This is good if you are being chased by a tiger. Tiger Schmiger! There are no tigers – especially not in our classrooms. Yet, children are responding to psychological anxiety that is as real as a real tiger.

The body and brain respond as if there is imminent danger. Access to logical processing or higher-order mathematical calculations is cut off in favor of survival. Working Memory is eliminated and, therefore, the child's foundational circuits for doing even rudimentary adding or subtracting are unavailable.

Opposing cortisol, we have neurotransmitters. These chemical messengers are how the brain communicates neuron-to-neuron, circuit-to-circuit. Without enough of the "feel-good" chemicals, we experience behaviors linked to deficiencies. For instance, a shortage of serotonin will leave the child sad and anxious. By decreasing cortisol in the learning space and increasing neurotransmitters, we enable a happy child, ready to learn.

Ball Drop

You can change the cortisol effect – simply eliminate cortisol from your class and introduce several positive neurotransmitters that make learning fun for all children.

We can create classroom activities that deliver not only serotonin, but also other neurotransmitters that fuel learning, like dopamine, norepinephrine, and oxytocin.

Ball Drop is an easy classroom activity to pump up the fun and infuse neurotransmitters into your classroom.

How to Do it

1. Two children stand one in front of the other with hands outstretched.
2. The first child holds two tennis (or lacrosse) balls in their hands, palms turned down. Child #2 then places their outstretched hands half-inch over the hands that are about to drop the balls.
3. When Child #1 drops the balls, Child #2 tries to catch them before they hit the floor.
4. Even if they fail, oxytocin (team building, sense of belonging), norepinephrine (anticipation, focus, concentration), dopamine (success, fun, happy), and serotonin (fun, sense of friendship, feel-good) changes the energy in the classroom.

> 💡 This game works, even for bystanders. All children in the room will be positively affected by the boost in helpful neurotransmitters putting them in their PFC and ready to reason and learn.

What's the Big Idea?

When the lesson is over and the children transition to a different place (physically or intellectually) there is only one question to answer: "What enduring Big Idea did the children walk away with?"

If the teacher didn't intentionally establish the big idea before the lesson, it is unlikely that children will walk away understanding it.

Big Ideas are like anchors – they establish meaningful connections between stray scraps of information so that the mind can make sense of them together. Without that anchor, the stray scraps of information would be inert, and not very useful beyond taking up space in our working memory.

When a teacher makes sense of information in schemas that are accessible to children, that's when learning happens.

What's Really Happening?

It is difficult for many kids to grasp ideas about time and place unless it relates to them, at that moment. We call this "**Me Here Now.**" This is often due to limitations of our working memory (adjusted Miller's Law) which is defined as 3 plus/minus 2. When we choose to work at the lower condition (1 item of information) and relate new material to "Me Here Now," all children will be able to manipulate (with ease) at least *one* new concept in working memory. Assuming that children arrive to class with extraneous issues that take up their brain space, we know that anchoring new information to one Big Idea will favor all children in their capacity to access new information, regardless of difficulty or complexity.

When we connect two supporting items to the Big Idea, this allows us to connect many more related concepts (as long as each new concept is routed through the supporting scaffold and focuses fully on the Big Idea). For example, the date 1969 is a Big Idea that contains a huge amount of information about landing the first human on the moon.

Consolidate the Big Idea with LTP

LTP (long-term potentiation) causes children to focus their thinking on a single item: a word, a phrase, or a drawing that serves to "make visible" their thinking.

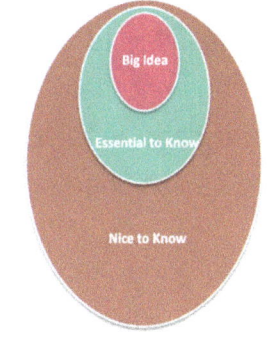

The advantage of using LTP as the Big Idea is that you are being intentional about providing real-time and long-lasting cognitive rehearsal that promotes enduring learning.

The more times a child can practice cognitive rehearsal, the more myelin develops, and the more connections to circuits in white matter occur. This leads to a deeper understanding.

When a child finds their voice and is able to articulate one Big Idea based on "Me Here Now," there is an immediate and long-lasting sense of belonging to the class, to the teacher, to the cohort, and to the content.

How to Do it

1. At the end of your lesson, ask the children to write or draw something that captures what this new information means to them.
2. Continue the theme the next day. Begin by inviting each child to share their word or drawing to state why they chose that particular anchor to describe their feeling.
3. Conduct this exercise without any rewards, punishments, editorializing, or distractions of any kind, so that each child finds their voice and articulates their thoughts.

💡 The Nested Egg illustrates how a Big Idea protects the child's working memory to avoid cognitive overload.

Left in the Dust

It happens. A child is left in the dust. Classmates can move rapidly ahead with constructs and concepts that seem easy and accessible to them, but other children are not able to make sense of them. A teacher might be prompted to think that the child who is falling behind is just not able and should be assigned special treatment.

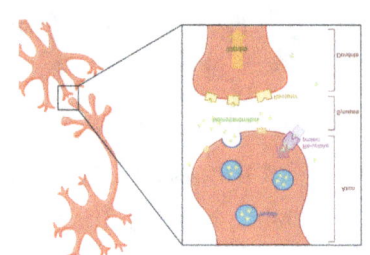

Sometimes a student is not able to grasp a new concept or abstract construct. It is not their fault. They need the white matter structures to be in place first. A neural lens points out that the child might not yet have had the opportunity to grow structures and myelinate new pathways that facilitate the new material.

What's Really Happening?

Long-term potentiation is probably the most important neural method that you introduce to your teaching practice to keep all children moving forward with ease. Here is how it works:

Incoming sensory information generates a perceptive experience. This is manifested by a circuit of neurons firing together. Think about a warm breeze that bristles some hairs on your arm. Immediately, sensory information is delivered to your brain so that you can perceive the breeze and its defining elements. Involuntarily, you recall other warm breezes that bring back memories and experiences from a time and place in your past. You might even remember people and feelings associated with that breezy perceptive experience.

Every time these neurons fire together, the original experience is re-generated. Over time and with frequent synchrony, this circuit of neurons becomes permanently sensitized. When one fires, they all fire. This is long-term potentiation in action (a strengthening of synaptic connections).

LTP Strengthens Working Memory

Setting an intention is critical when it comes to LTP. This exercise gives educators a set format to grow white matter tracts for their students in areas of the brain that use working memory, comprehension, and deep understanding.

This exercise uses an intentional moment to create a memory, then the power of sleep to solidify it.

Neuronal activation works in synchrony. In this exercise, *every* student learns at the same time, through each other's experiences. The best part is that the synchrony of neuronal connections that occurred during the lesson on the previous day, was *already present* for the child as they shared their experience on the following day.

How to Do it

1. End a lesson with a short activity: each child writes a word or phrase and/or draws something that celebrates the lesson.
2. Children sleep that night (ideally 8-10 hours).
3. The next day, begin the lesson (continued theme) by inviting each child to share their writing or drawing and state what they chose and why they chose it. Listen without interrupting, editorializing, or commenting.
4. When finished, ask the speaker to choose the next classmate to share their word or drawing, until all children have had an opportunity to share.

💡 Make sure that all children are invited to share and their voices are heard to help them articulate their thoughts.

Cognitive Load

Cognitive load is the amount of information that working memory can hold at one time. At the best of times, this spatial measure is pretty tiny (like memorizing a new phone number as you are trying to dial it).

More importantly, working memory can be impacted by a person, place or thing that interrupts to impose unnecessary demands on a learner. Everything from distractions to sensory stimulation can introduce new cognitive demands. In addition, what happened at home, in the cafeteria, on the playground, or on the journey to or from school, can also take up that precious processing space.

Think of it this way: a child's working memory is to the brain's full potential 'as a coffee cup is to fifteen times the number of stars in the Milky Way.'

What's Really Happening?

In 1956, information systems scientist George Miller attempted to quantify the limitations of human working memory. According to his calculations, *Homo sapiens* could manage 7+/-2 (5 to 9) pieces of incoming information at a time. Today, we know he overshot the mark. This was pointed out by Herbert Simon who was convinced that 7 "bits" was way too high. Miller's study was replicated in 2010 and verified that Simon was closer to the truth with a number approaching 3 +/- 2 (1 - 5).

Most children are already stressed and hyper-vigilant, just trying to juggle 21st century information tsunamis, gadgets, chores, homework, and social media. It's no wonder that these children struggle to add even more to their working memory by learning even just 1 or 2 new constructs in a classroom.

From Automaticity to Cognitive Load

When learners know something well, their working memory is freed up for interpreting and managing other incoming sensory information. For instance, 2+2 is so simple that it takes up a negligible cognitive load. But multiplying 798 X 357 is a different matter.

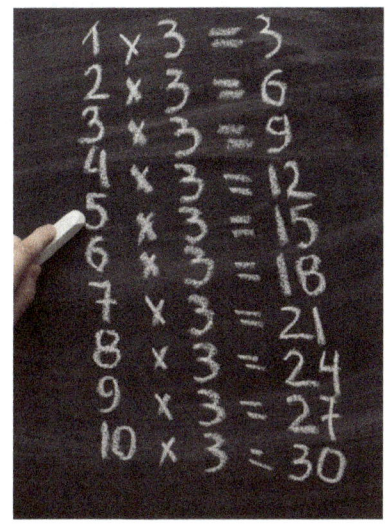

In the learning space, teachers can be intentional about growing and strengthening the learner's working memory, by utilizing methods that take a child from automaticity to cognitive load and back again.

This exercise works best when the child has an opportunity to remain in an *intrinsic motivation status* – that means acting with autonomy, mastery, and purpose. In defining the lesson, look for ways to give them a choice (but keep it simple). By introducing manageable chunks, the child will experience immediate mastery and with the autonomy and mastery be able to align with a useful purpose.

How to Do it

1. Begin with a series on the number line, such as: 0, 5, 10, 15, 20, and so on up to 100.

2. When the learner is comfortable with this exercise and derives a sense of mastery at arriving at one hundred, move to a new number sequence (6s or 7s).

3. The cognitive load will be higher for a number like 7. If the child struggles, return to a number like 5 and they'll notice how easy it seems. Remind them that it wasn't always easy for them. There was a time when counting by 5s was hard too, and they can learn to count with as much ease by 7s or any other number.

💡 Moving from automaticity to cognitive load and back helps strengthen brain structures.

Imposter Syndrome

Imposter syndrome is more common than one might think, especially in schools. It occurs when an individual doubts their skills, talents, or accomplishments. Imposter syndrome has a persistent internalized fear of being exposed as a fraud.

Children who are overcome with imposter syndrome might worry that their friends will find out that they aren't smart enough. At the same time, they often think that they do not deserve good grades and that the B+ they got for math or science was merely an accident.

When the child doubts their accomplishments, they easily see the teacher's red marks as confirming that indeed they are not worthy of the higher grades that other kids can achieve. A child can thus remain in a downward spiral.

What's Really Happening?

When a child has low self-esteem, they see their failure and downward spiral as an internal issue. It's their fault. They can also see it as a general characteristic of their personality: "I'm hopeless at school." They believe this as fact and their internal fault-finding global hopelessness is something that cannot change. This is the Fixed Mindset.

Without understanding how their **Reticular Activating System** works, it's difficult for them to see beyond this fixed state. When good things happen, the child will not be able to see it as real. Instead, they'll see it as a one-time fluke that won't happen again. Or, they might think that the success only applied to that one specific thing. Sometimes, the child will concede the win to help they received, or the helper themselves.

It is therefore crucial to teach the child foundational concepts about their own brain and how they can embrace a growth mindset to show up in the world.

Purposeful Mastery

Teaching methods that focus on positive tangible outcomes should become classroom norms.

Sometimes, we create opportunities for children to work with other children who already know the material where the child is lagging. However, we find that this technique works even better when we also pair the child with someone who knows even less than them.

Together, the children figure out how to ask questions and how to find answers to questions that they didn't even know existed earlier.

Finally, when all else fails, create a fun oxytocin gift-wrapped learning event that contains both cognitive load and small-motor skill components. This targets the skill and the white matter structure that the child needs to myelinate in order to become proficient – and soon expert – in this area.

How to Do it

1. Simplify your rubrics so the child can access their reasoning brain. Invite the student to achieve meaningful quality chunks that are possible to complete in a short time so they can see tangible, meaningful mastery.

2. Know the child's purpose and discuss this with them, not the objective of the lesson. It is easy to connect any work with a child's purpose in life or their dreams to forge a path to achievement.

💡 All children have dreams. Connect their dreams with achievable mastery and purpose.

Learned Helplessness

"When I don't succeed at a task, I find myself blaming my own stupidity for my failure. I feel that anyone else could be better than me at most tasks. I feel that I have little control over the outcomes of my work."

How many times have you heard these or similar things from your students? Children are not born with a mindset that includes the above three items. Yet, we find children in schools every day who could have said these same statements.

Learned helplessness occurs when a child experiences a sense of powerlessness, usually from persistent failure to succeed. A child can receive excessive corrective measures, red marks, reminders, and criticism.

The brain is malleable - the younger the child the more plastic it is. It makes no sense that a child would learn helplessness at home or at school, yet it is a reality.

What's Really Happening?

From a neurobiological standpoint, every child will have genetic predispositions from their biological parents. Genetic factors establish the child in the world. Epigenetic factors influence how the child interacts in that world. Genes are expressed for children based on geography, culture, parenting styles, relationships, friendships, and emotional connections. These genetic gifts will include a factor that can wield a powerful influence on learning and interacting with life in school and later in life - a measure of **Autonomic Nervous System (ANS) reactivity**.

ANS reactivity is a measure of sensitivity (or resilience) to events in social contexts. A child might be considered *sensitive* or *not-so-sensitive* (resilient) on a continuum that stretches from high ANS reactivity to low ANS reactivity.

Expected Confidence

"I accept tasks even if I am not sure that I will succeed at them. I feel that my success reflects my ability, not chance. I am able to reach my goals in life."

This is the same child with a new mindset. The difference is astounding. Not because it is less negative, but because it sets the child up for success throughout life.

The one big influence for turning on or off genes related to ANS reactivity, is the social context. That's where you come in.

Social contexts occur in the home, playground, cafeteria, your classroom, school hallways, or anywhere a child interacts with others. You can help the children who have difficulties navigating any, or all, of these social contexts by using social contexts to reduce their ANS reactivity.

How to Do it

1. Teach the child that behind every behavior is a message from the brain. All behavior is simply communication.
2. Co-create your classroom so that the child feels invested in and part of the learning space and its events.
3. Put yourself in the place of the child. Walk into your lesson with their fears and ability. Can you see yourself in this lesson? Is it safe, fun, and inviting?

💡 Every child has a different level of susceptibility to social context. Understanding this is key to making your classroom inviting for all children.

No Brain

Ask any teacher for their definition of learning and you will get as many definitions as people you ask. Why is this the case? Why is it so hard to define what we do every day in the classroom?

Most of the answers will have some aspect of the following — "knowledge acquired through teaching, experience, or practice."

When the end result is measured in grades and high-stakes testing systems, it makes sense that the definition would speak to "knowledge acquired," even though most teachers decry the entire memorization and regurgitation schedule.

In order for success in such a learning scenario, there has to be a keen desire for attentive compliance so that all children can listen for instructions, follow instructions, and turn in finished lessons in a timely manner. The trouble is, that's not how the learning brain works.

What's Really Happening?

When the focus is on academic output as measured in a competitive grading system, the teacher is toiling in an uneven playing field where at least 50% of children are disadvantaged. Classrooms that are designed to fit a behavior model are not amenable to diversity of any kind – neural, cultural, race, religion, age, gender, disability, and so on. Children who have never been taught to focus are immediately disadvantaged. Teachers who have never been taught about how the brain handles stress responses, or how children's brains learn, are also disadvantaged in such a scenario.

A simplistic model that outlines the neuroscience behind a **hierarchical brain** structure allows teachers to access methods and practices that eliminate biases, understand cognitive load, activate neural processing, and connect at a primal level with a child's learning brain.

Whole Brain

A child's brain consists of a cerebellum and four lobes. When we design lesson plans that include not just the frontal lobe, but the whole brain, we include all these learning centers and build structures that connect the regions.

It's not so much about the subject i.e., science, math, or history, but more about being able to use the subject matter to engage the child with exercises that architect the child's brain so that in life, they will know knowledge and have a strong architected brain to use that knowledge.

Neuroscience experts recently discovered that up to 70% of human neurons are in the **cerebellum** – the "small brain." In addition, they found that the cerebellum connects with and monitors the four other lobes: occipital (visual), temporal (speech), parietal (motor), and frontal (executive). Thus, engaging the cerebellum and the four lobes allows the child to access more information, process more knowledge, and gain a deeper understanding.

How to Do it

1. Teach all children about their own brains; if they can remember 10,000 Pokemon characters, they can learn ten things about their brains that will change their lives.

2. It is not so simple as connecting the teacher's executive region with the child's executive region. First, you must connect your executive region with the child's survival region. Then, you can engage executive higher-order functions together.

3. Whole brain is a required approach for designing brain-based lessons. Activate the cerebellum with movement, activate the occipital lobe with visuals, activate the temporal lobe with music and song, and so on.

💡 When you include the whole brain in your lessons, each learner is drawn in.

Pedagogy

It is not good enough to know *what*; we also need to understand *how*. This is a critical layer that sits between the content knowledge and the consumer of that content knowledge – the learner.

As teachers, we suffer from too much content and too little time. While this is in fact very true, it is not necessarily the optimal measure of understanding what teaching means. Such a vision of learning ends up with an education that is "a mile wide and an inch deep."

Instead of focusing on content (what), we should focus on who and how, i.e., children and how their brains work. It is essential to be intentional about building strong relationships with each individual learner. Too often a child will associate hating math or science because they think the teacher hates them or they hate the teacher. Hate is a strong word and penetrates deep into the limbic region.

What's Really Happening?

All children can learn. But we live in a multi-sensory world; the child's brain is constantly being bombarded by stimulation from sounds, sights, touch, smells, and tastes. Each individual has a remarkable capacity to inhibit irrelevant information and create meaning with relevant sensory information.

Children are essentially goal-directed beings who thrive in intrinsically-motivated activities. Innate intrinsic motivation is derived from an inner dominant altruistic feeling, with an innate desire and ability to make a contribution and experience a sense of belonging through participatory fun and social interaction.

As such, school shouldn't be something that is "happening" to children. Rather, they excel when they can *choose* to be part of a learning environment that includes and respects their voice and contribution.

A Pedagogic Model

Instead of content, let's focus on schemas. A schema is used to organize knowledge and guide cognitive processes. Schemas are critical for making sense of our multi-sensory, experiential world. In the classroom, teachers co-create meaningful schemas so that learners can access and consume relevant information from multiplicities of incoming sensory information.

Pedagogic models are everywhere in education. Some are better than others for some children – one size does not fit all. A brain-based pedagogic model aligns with how the human brain works and how all children learn.

There are three major pillars of pedagogy in this brain-based model: Disequilibrium (Piaget), chunking (Miller), and cognitive rehearsal (Hebb). The child will discover new information in a way that keeps their brain growing (plasticity) and activates their memory through Long-Term Potentiation.

How to Do it

1. Disequilibrium is a simple effective way to cause attentional arousal, conceptual change, fun, and personalized understanding.
2. Chunking, or delivering information in small chunks, allows children (who have tiny working memory systems) to access concepts more easily. When they do, they'll generate ideas and contribute to the work. Positive neurotransmitters will produce personal satisfaction that encourages them to seek out more learning experiences.
3. Cognitive rehearsal helps children achieve simple mastery so they are wired to seek out more and more complex concepts. Think leveling up from gaming.

💡 Using schemas over memorization-regurgitation makes learning possible for all children.

The Phenotype Child

It's Tuesday evening. Suddenly, Mom realizes it is 10 PM and no one is prepping for bed. She looks at the two children and notices, in frustration, that once again they are not close to being ready for sleep time. She launches an onslaught on her two children:

"Look at the time. Ten o'clock! You've got school in the morning. Do you hear me? Stop texting and put that phone away."

Mary is a resilient child, with low ANS reactivity. She goes to bed and sleeps soundly and wakes up ready for school. Peter is a different phenotype with high ANS reactivity. He goes to bed, cries himself to sleep, and thinks Mom "hates" him like he hates school.

Why is it that two children conceived of the same parents, born into the same family, growing up in the same neighborhoods, and attending the same schools could be so different, and ultimately experience such dramatic differences in life?

What's Really Happening?

Resilience is how quickly one can bounce back after an emotional setback. Some children can shrug it off and recover quickly; other children tend to sink into prolonged negative spirals. The first one looks like a delicate orchid, which will wilt unless the environment is adjusted. The other resembles a hardy dandelion, which can survive even in a crack in the concrete.

Children who are less resilient in a social context have what is called high **Autonomic Nervous System (ANS)** reactivity. Psychological safety is predicted by a child's ANS reactivity. Self-regulation is strongly tied to acceptance and understanding of one's own ANS reactivity.

When parents or teachers are unaware of differing phenotypes in children's makeup, they almost always say and do the exact wrong thing to exacerbate a crisis.

Regulation for Reason

How might mom have better dealt with bedtime, given the diversity in autonomic nervous system reactivity in her children? Mom needs to stay in her rational brain.

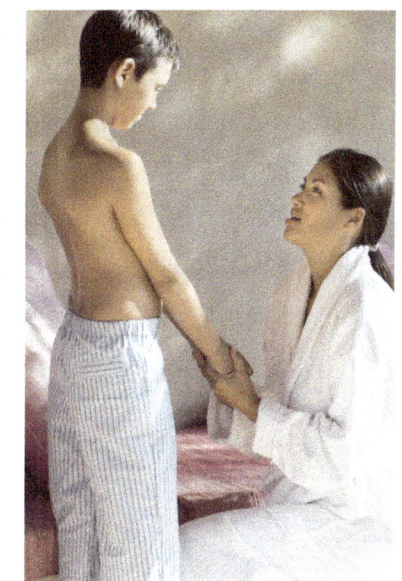

Of course, children do not come with ANS reactivity scores or guidebooks. But, if mom was aware of the neuroscience behind why some children are more or less resilient, she might have had a different approach – and a very different outcome.

If you have never thought about your ANS reactivity, there is a high probability that you will have difficulty self-regulating. When we teach children the vocabulary and mental models relating to a continuum between resilience and sensitivity, they are able to co-regulate with you first, then self-regulate.

How to Do it

1. Self-regulate yourself before addressing a problem with children. Take a deep breath, hold it and count to 5, then exhale.

2. Explain the situation in a kind and gentle way. Mom could have said, "Bedtime in the deVerolm household. Where are my beautiful children? Mary, you have swim lessons in the morning. Do you want help with your lunch? Please wind down your texting and say good night to Louise." Then, "Peter, soccer game! I am so excited to see you play tomorrow. How close you came to scoring last week. I am so proud of you."

3. Study the "blossoming flower" metaphor: when an orchid wilts, we do not change the orchid, we change the environment (water, temperature, or soil pH). Similarly, when we see a child unable to learn (wilting) we change the environment, change the access point, information chunking, assessment, the challenge.

💡 A different approach gets a different outcome.

I Need Proof

We can't actually see white matter structures unless we have very expensive imaging equipment. However, it is possible to see the results of growing white matter structures within a few minutes or a few hours. Many teachers want proof that brain-based practices work. Proof that you can help your students grow new white matter structures.

What's Really Happening?

Proof is everywhere. If you can ride a bike, then at some point you would have had to grow the "bike-riding" white matter structure in your brain. You weren't born with it already in place! Think about what it takes to ride a bike. Balance, eyes on the horizon, downward force on pedals, coordination, turning, speeding up, slowing down, stopping. It's a lot to take in at once. Yet, we can do this seamlessly without any cognitive load because we built the circuit for bike riding, and myelinated it with cognitive rehearsal - at first with the help of some adult and later alone. In appetitive learning situations, we follow the child's appetite. Structures follow.

When school is fun, children are not only invited to the party, but they are also willing to get out on the floor and dance. Creating activities that engender fun creates an appetite for learning. Appetite increases Aptitude.

Circuit Synchrony

This project helps build an entirely new structure through circuit synchrony, just like you did when you learned to ride a bike. For this exercise, we'll use ball bouncing to create rhythm in a small group.

In the exercise, some children bring agility with soccer balls, rugby balls, or tennis balls. They might be inclined to dominate and take the lead role, moving at a pace that causes other children to want to drop out. This is an opportunity to validate that all children can acquire structures that allow them to contribute.

How to Do it

1. Set the stage. You'll need two soccer-shaped inflated balls so that they bounce easily and responsively. Choose a space to practice your routine.

2. Review examples of others doing the exercise. It helps clarify the process if someone shows them examples on YouTube or other groups' attempts. It's not important that they be polished; in fact mistakes and disasters are welcome.

3. Use two balls of any size to create a rhythmic event with a small group. Children decide what rhythm they would like to create with bouncing balls. Sometimes, one of the children will use only hand or foot clapping to change the sound effect. What they create is not so important, as long as they come together and decide as a group and document their efforts over time.

4. Give each child the chance to iterate the exercise at least five or six times, learning each time from the earlier attempts. As they document their journey, they are essentially documenting the growth of the white matter circuits that will be in place when they are ready to go public. Cognitive rehearsal leads to myelinated connections which deliver fluency in mental models, automaticity in physical activities, and neurotransmitters for success.

💡 Synchronous firing of neuronal structures will result in long-term potentiation so that the child will gain facility, command of vocabulary, and dexterity with the balls.

Words Count

The trouble with words is that meaning is implied. If I say I am happy, I am assuming that you know the same meaning of happy as I do. Your "happy" might be (and should be) very different from mine. That's because we each have our own unique brains. Just like fingerprints, no two brains are the same.

Unfortunately, we tend to assume that we all know the same meaning. This applies particularly to children who might not have had a lot of exposure to new vocabulary or advanced constructs that require deep understanding.

Let's start with the word "focus." The teacher will direct the children to "pay attention" or to "focus." Then when it is obvious that the children are not focusing like the teacher expected, there seems to be no alternative but punishment. Pay attention, or else!

What's Really Happening?

Is it wrong to assume that the child has no inkling about what focus means? Consider the anthropologist who is learning the language and customs of a tribe in New Guinea for the first time. How surprised he is when he discovers that the language has no word for counting. It matters not if there are seven objects or sixteen objects; it only matters that they know that one amount is smaller (or larger) than the other.

It works the same for our children. Unless someone has taken the time to explain and show them what it means to focus, we shouldn't assume that they already know the construct. Being able to focus is a skill that is representative of a white matter neural structure, which has been established and myelinated over time in each individual. How you focus should, and probably does, differ from how I focus.

How you focus when writing, or watching a favorite show, or while filling out your IRS tax form might all be quite different. Yet, it works every time.

Focus

Each child will need the white matter structure for focus as they progress through school. If the teacher is kind, and if the child is shown how to focus and given lots of opportunities to make mistakes at focusing, they will walk away with a good understanding and a skill for life.

As children observe, take notes, and articulate what is happening while classmates pay attention during the execution of a task, they are essentially forging those white matter tracts that facilitate an understanding of focus. Then, when they themselves are completing a task, they will be able to recognize their own method for paying attention. This is how they begin to understand what focus means.

As each child listens to and grasps what others are saying when they describe focus, they are able to see how the focus is different for most people and yet they all seem to get the task completed because they were able to pay attention and hold that attention over time.

How to Do it

1. All children will benefit from this exercise; it's important not to isolate and publicly place attention on children who appear to not be focused. Children's bodies do not all look the same when they are focused.
2. Invite any child to, instead of doing a designated task, observe children in a group and note how they approach focus.
3. When the task is complete, invite everyone to listen to the observer share what was happening, individual by individual, so that it becomes obvious what focus looks like.

💡 Rotate through the group each time to ensure everyone has a chance to show their focus.

Memory is Fasciculus

It happens to all of us. "Where did I put my keys?" or "I know that lady...but I can't for the life of me think of her name?" We struggle every day to remember bits and pieces of our lives. Even when we are deliberate about always placing the keys on the key rack, or making a mental note about the time of a certain event, we find ourselves more often than we would like, in a situation where we have to rack our brains to retrieve a memory.

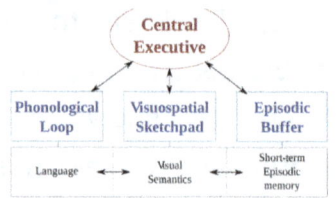

In school, it looks like this: the teacher spends inordinate amounts of time reminding children of due dates, how to complete an assignment, where an event must happen, and what time to be there. It's never ending. And it never seems to improve. The same children are the same forgetful kiddos who need these reminders day in and day out. So what's going on?

What's Really Happening?

Memory is universal. We often break it into two simple buckets: short- and long-term. But memory is more complex than that. Short-term memory is like a buffer in working memory, giving us the capacity to recall a few items for immediate application. For instance, you might focus intensely by repeating a few digits to keep a number alive while dialing. But there are other types of memory:

Episodic Memory: reconstruct recent or past experiences

Semantic Memory: non-personal, factual

Procedural Memory: skills learned – body remembers how to

Implicit Memory: unconscious automatic memories

The big take-away for educators is that memory is malleable. Your own and your students' memories can improve. Many easy and quick techniques can help children grow their working memory and improve their capacity for retention. You can improve the speed and efficiency of the **Central Executive's** connection to language and visual semantics by doing specific exercises with the student in the **phonological loop** and the **visuospatial sketchpad**.

Play for Memory

Fun games and challenges that engage critical brain structures will foster strong memory and deep understanding.

The **phonological loop** consists of neuronal structures that connect circuits in Broca's and Wernicke's areas involving speech and understanding.

The **visuospatial sketchpad** involves areas of the brain that connect frontal executive structures with parietal integrative and occipital visual circuitry.

When these concepts are paired with predictable, consistent, and kind aerobic exercise activities, children make memories. This activates relevant receptors in the hippocampus and increases exercise-induced brain-derived neurotrophic factor (BDNF). BDNF fosters neurogenesis and enhances neuroplasticity.

How to Do it

1. Play with word ladders, dictionary games, and thesauruses so that children can get lost and make mistakes in the phonological loop.

2. Introduce a week-long project where all students find their home or favorite park on a map of the school environs; every individual traces their journey from home to school.

3. Motivation connects directly with the visuospatial sketchpad when it involves autonomy, opportunities for mastery, and a general sense of purpose.

💡 It is easy to grow white matter myelinated structures for speech and understanding.

Mental Models for UDL

When you encounter a child who is obviously in an amygdala hijack (aggressive or oppositional behavior), your mindset might be: "She won't stop..." or "he is deliberately flouting my authority."

Instead of thinking that the student was acting in such a disruptive way out of choice, notice what happens to your thinking when you recognize the behavior as an involuntary reaction beyond the child's choice.

Now we are in the zone of regulation.

Universal Design for Learning (UDL) is a framework that reflects how a child's brain engages with learning spaces and social contexts for optimal access and outcomes.

Many of the constructs that are surfaced in a model-like UDL are already in the classroom, and it is often surprising that teachers realize that a small tweak can access the full power of these engaging models.

What's Really Happening?

As teachers, we know from our research in neuroscience, that a child in an amygdala hijack is reacting from a part of the brain where there is no access to higher-order functioning, decision-making, predicting, and logical thinking. So why would we think that such a brain would be able to calm down, or be able to respond to "Don't ..." instructions? In reality, the child may not hear the instructions. Auditory functions can be overridden by the hyperactive amygdala.

Children are not born with the ability to regulate their behavior. Regulation (especially self-regulation) requires consistent activation of structures that connect the amygdalae, hippocampi, and frontal lobe networks that are associated with inhibition.

Greenhouse

By the time we reach adulthood we should be able to self-regulate, although certain stressors might trigger behavior that we might revisit later in frustration. It's true – the amygdala can still let us down at the most inopportune moments.

When the child is experiencing a meltdown, screaming, and kicking, we can recognize these outbursts as the perfect practice for co-regulating. Rather than "Oh no, here we go again," think, "This is the moment I have been waiting for."

As an adult in the learning space, you cannot afford to also be in an amygdala hijack. This is not a time to try to reason, or remind the child of the zero-tolerance consequences for bad behavior. It's a time for deep breathing, mirror neurons, and calm supportive leadership.

How to Do it

1. Reason works for children when we provide the opportune moment to reflect on how the brain reacts to stressors. Plan ahead; make room for community circles to discuss stress.

2. Allow time for mirror neurons to take effect. Children who play in the vocabulary of escalation, de-escalation, mirror neurons and support, can become leaders that can access reason.

3. Constructs that convey feelings and supports are accessible to all brains within reason. Expect excellence in behavior, imaginative support systems with peers and fun.

💡 A simple mind shift regarding behavior can make a huge impact on regulation.

Fear of Math

Vocabulary is key to understanding. New terms and novel constructs of a mathematical nature, will be difficult for children who have not yet had enough opportunity to play (and make lots of mistakes) in the **visuospatial sketchpad**. Being allowed to make mistakes in a safe environment is very different from making mistakes in a hostile, social-evaluative threatening and/or competitive environment.

Children who are familiar with arithmetic verbiage and related methods and constructs, will breeze through new material. Meanwhile, children who have not had the opportunity to grow the structures in the visual-spatial sketchpad that allows for such processing might struggle, give up easily, and become reactive during math class. It is therefore essential to set them up with pertinent vocabulary and time they need to grow these white matter structures.

What's Really Happening?

When you cause the brain to activate well-trodden myelinated pathways towards primal survival, as opposed to fun engaging new opportunities, you will get these reactive results every time. When the amygdala directs incoming sensory information to the reactive brain, the child will act with an involuntary freeze, fight, flight, and/or fawn response.

"I'm no good at math..." is a thinking that stems from a firm belief, which begins and ends with the Reticular Activating System (**RAS**). Recall that it is the job of the RAS to confirm our beliefs all day, every day. It is not only efficient; RAS is deadly accurate. A teacher might assume that a child is receiving solid "feedback" with reminders and criticism for their benefit. But their RAS is convinced that you are confirming that they are, in fact, *no good at math*. They translate the corrective Red Marks, your Body Language and words to mean that you too, know that they are no good at math. It's a constant punishment - **Sisyphus** pushing a rock uphill forever – a journey with no reprieve and no light at the end of the tunnel.

Deep Learning

Fear of learning can change when you use a pedagogic model that allows a child to engage in higher-order frontal lobe processing.

When we teach to the brain, the child will thrive. Learners are able to take advantage of a co-created, psychologically safe, learning environment that is inclusive, welcoming, and fun. Children will no longer fear subjects like math!

What used to be negative, begins to shift to a tentative positive trial: *I used to think I was no good at math, but since I figured out that anyone can learn math, I am improving every day.*

How to Do it

1. Don't delay. Play with mathematical vocabulary early and often. Make it fun!
2. Every day, show the child they have improved mastery at simple calculations that are appropriate for age and skill level. Be intentional about feedback. Avoid using red marks. Math too, can be predictable, consistent, and kind.
3. If the child lags behind, you might have to begin with fundamentals and take time to set in place strong foundational structures that will stay for a lifetime.

💡 All children *can* do math, just like they can read, write, and play ball. Use positive RAS reinforcement and vocabulary to help each child discover their ability.

Deliberate Behavior in Social Gatherings

The RAS is our filtering system - it decides what critical information to bring to our conscious awareness. It is easy to wire our **Reticular Activating Systems (RAS)** in the faculty room, the hallways, or at the after-work coffee catch-up. These breaks from engagement on the front lines are welcome and important.

But let's consider the conversations in these areas. Educators are often overworked, weary, and stressed – fresh from difficult classroom encounters. They may say that a certain child is oppositional, or "just doesn't want to...he is being manipulative and doesn't care."

Our RAS and mental models are driven by vocabulary. Brain-based mental models can override the entrenched verbiage that one often hears at these gatherings of educators, by reminding us that all behavior is communication from the brain.

What's Really Happening?

Vocabulary starts the ball rolling. When an educator includes concepts and constructs like **short-term memory**, **intentional hippocampal neurogenesis**, and **long-term potentiation**, that educator is not stuck in entrenched thinking systems that consider behavior as two-dimensional (either "good" or "bad").

Many of the labels attributed to learners can be accepted as a full description of who that child is and the potential for their life journey. In reality, haphazard labels do not tell us all we need to know about any child as they pursue their learning journey with us.

Involuntary Reaction Drives Behavior

Mental models drive our thinking. This thinking informs our actions and, in particular, our reactions.

There is an important difference between the mental model that comes from, "He's obnoxious, ill-mannered, and offensive…" and the understanding that, "It is a difficult challenge, because he has already myelinated some pretty aggressive and obnoxious defense mechanisms, which he certainly didn't pick up in my classroom. And I am willing to be one of the four consistently caring adults in his life."

From the brain's point of view, it is perfectly plausible for a stressor to cause a person to refuse to cooperate, to not comply, and to always not make a "right" choice.

As the adult in the child's life, it is easy to discover how to change the environment so that any child can thrive.

How to Do it

1. Tell yourself that students do well if they *can*. That means you might need to support this child in the face of other educators and parents saying negative things about them. We appreciate the work of Dr Ross Green for these useful insights.
2. Remember that all students want to do well. They do not get up in the morning and decide to do "awful" today, or to make some teacher's life miserable.
3. Help a child experience mastery at something that they like to do, and grow that feeling of success and potential.

💡 Children want to do well, and do well when they *can*. It's an educator's job to create an environment where all children *can*.

I am still learning...

- Michelangelo at 87

Epilogue

While intuition succeeded in the past; reason consolidates the knowing

Any child failing to reach their true potential is frustrating to a teacher who knows the promise of neural plasticity, equity, and educational opportunity in a world of limitless possibilities. Understanding neural plasticity tells us that every child has access to trillions upon trillions of white matter structures that enhance their learning capacity. We also know that a child's brain is not a child's destiny.

All this should mean that foundational knowledge of neuroscience, access to tech-enabled pedagogies, and modern learning systems, should deliver a future where our children thrive in schools and develop a lifelong and enduring love of learning.

But knowledge alone is not enough. Schools are jam-packed with materials and content, yet equally jammed with children who are overwhelmed, stressed and unable to keep up. Methods work best when they are grounded in practice that is informed by neural approaches. Neural approaches allow teachers and students access to their working memory, their emotional midbrains, and especially their rational higher-order thinking brains. The shift happens first for teachers; a shift from scope and sequence to being mindful of the child's appetite. Appetite is opposite to aptitude. From the brain's standpoint appetite comes first...aptitude follows.

This is not easy. A school's *raison d'être* is to deliver content - lots of content. Reputations are made and lost depending on content delivery. Schools and teachers are often measured by how well this content is delivered, absorbed and regurgitated by children in high-stakes tests. Teachers are thus judged by success at managing scope and sequence. Sadly, that can translate into a teacher's ability to keep children's focus and attention on a prescribed academic topic for a given amount of time.

Unfortunately, such an approach makes very little sense to the learning brain - in fact, it can easily lead to cognitive overload, stress, boredom (which is another form of stress), and ultimately and progressively to disengagement. Even more unfortunately, in some traditional models for teaching and learning, disengagement is often met with threats, token economies, bribes, public shaming, punishments, and frustration.

At the same time, the shift is easy and manageable. It's always easy in hindsight - so, walk with me. It's just words.

Simply put, we begin with vocabulary; we re-invent through mindset, and we follow a child's passion. Passion is appetite in emotional pedigree. By following a child's appetite, we discover their particular aptitude. In emotional language we look for *affect* first and then grow *effect*. Affect is feeling; effect can be results - even grades. This kind of thinking draws a less stringent border around scope and sequence.

In the old way, a teacher would find out what children loved and use it to reward or punish them, in order to consolidate a behavior that was desired. This worked roughly 50% of the time. It never worked for some percentage of children. Today, we know why these numbers hold true. When we approach our profession from the standpoint of autonomic nervous system reactivity and amygdala hijack, we can easily understand the consequences of using such an outdated pedagogy.

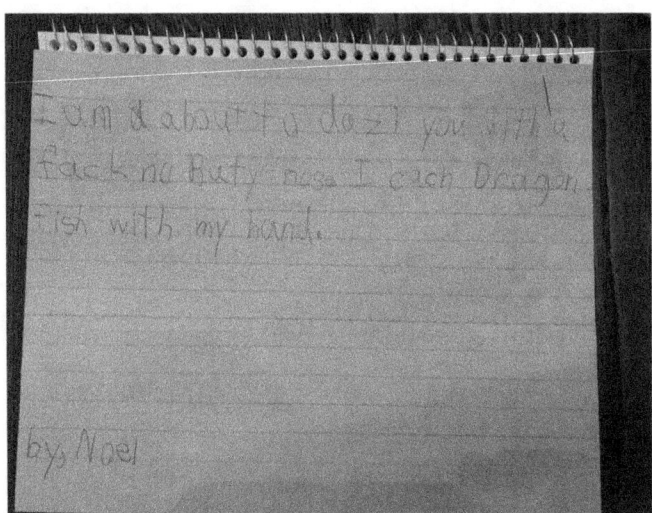

When a boy writes a report like the one shown here, to his teachers... we recognize an opportunity in the realm of appetite, passion and affect.

"I am about to dazzle you with a fact that nobody knows. I catch Dragon Fish with my hand"...

This child is clearly making visible his passion and desire to let his teachers know his feelings. Let's investigate a couple scenarios out of the myriad that could be enacted.

Scenario One: teacher can't (or won't) read it because the grammar is so bad and the child is obviously just seeking attention. Just as sad is... teacher reads it, tut tut's (or marks with **RED** pen) the grammar and dismisses the work.

Scenario Two: teacher reads the dazzling fact. Reads it with the boy and asks him to explain it in more detail. Asks probing questions: When did you catch the Dragon Fish? Where were you? Who was with you? How did you feel about it? How did it happen? Will you do it again? And so on.

In each scenario, the outcome will be very different for both the teacher and the boy. In both scenarios the brain will do its job - it will build and myelinate white matter structures in the hippocampus, amygdala and visual tracts that connect with the prefrontal rational thinking executive center. As these structures consolidate with sleep and more storified memories, they will have real meaning for behavior.

From the boy's point of view, the encounter with the teacher's reaction to his poorly written but passionate report, will teach him very valuable lessons.

In Scenario One, he might learn that it is meaningless and even bad to have passion about something that is not directly connected to right or wrong answers in school work. He will remember why he hates school. He will also learn that his teacher, whom he trusted with this very important information about his most meaningful passion, cannot be trusted in the future with anything - ever. And he also hates her subject - math, even though he is very good at math.

In Scenario Two, on the other hand, he might be so delighted and felt so included and supported, that he connects all his passions with school work and in particular with this teacher and especially, with her subject math. This he will carry with him for his entire life and will be able to recall long into his old age the feeling and the joy that he experienced on that day when the course of his future life was set.

The teacher might make a mental note that this boy is a troublemaker, just like she heard from other teachers in the faculty lounge. They confirm that he is always trying to insert extraneous bits of personal nonsense into her lesson to waste class time. She knows that when he gets reminders (which is a lot) he acts out and takes up even more time while she has to corral him. Sometimes, it's impossible to get him to attend like the other compliant children and he has to be sent to the quiet corner or to the principal's office.

The truth is, if a student doesn't have access to prefrontal cortex higher-order processing and executive function, they aren't able to engage, generate ideas, or contribute to the work at hand. They are defined by behaviors that are not congruent with teaching methods that are based on extrinsic modalities of reward and punishment.

What teachers do *after* becoming neural educators is find out what students are passionate about and what their dreams and plans are. They know that all children have dreams, plans and passions. Teachers make them visible so they can co-create their learning spaces and together fill their days with curiosity, new knowledge, deep understanding, and *joy*. Passionate, active learning ignites innovation, activates important neurotransmitters that enhance learning, builds trust, and fosters autonomy.

There is science to the power of connection for learning and engagement. When teachers harness this power, they change education for good.

The brain develops in a systematic way that reflects our evolutionary history. It starts from the bottom and builds towards the top. For this reason, we too begin at the bottom in a region that contains the brainstem and diencephalon. This is a primal survival region that evolved for Homo Sapiens and persists from an earlier evolutionary time. It is not a brain region that can engage in conscious thinking – it is characterized by reactive involuntary functions that elicit behaviors like freeze, flight, fight, and fawn.

Specialized structures in this part of the brain engage and activate survival schemas, as if your child were being chased by a tiger. Even though this is a very remote and dim prospect today that a child would be chased by a tiger in your classroom, the child's brain perceives stressors as this kind of danger. The very same fight-or-flight part of the brain that would save the child from a tiger is activated at the thought of "getting out those math Practical Guides." It is easy to understand why the usual classroom "go-to" solutions (like reprimanding and punishing children) have no meaning for a survival brain that cannot process conscious thinking.

As teachers, we anticipate this part of the child's survival brain because they show up dysregulated, causing them to engage in behavior that is ineffective for the learning space. It is good to remember that the adult cannot afford to also be dysregulated. As we attempt to de-escalate and co-regulate with our children, we must know how to, and be in, a state of self-regulation.

Higher up in the child's brain we encounter a "newer" evolutionary developmental state – the emotional brain – where the child can process happy, sad, angry, curious, and other powerful emotions that color their experiences. Once the child is feeling safe and calm, and knows that they are respected and loved, their limbic brain will be able to engage and activate structures that are already in place in relation to emotions that they recognize. New emotions will grow new structures as the experiences diversify and the child advances towards maturity. The opportunity to make mistakes and "do over" is a critical element in the myelination process of building solid emotional structures that will be in place for the child's living experiences.

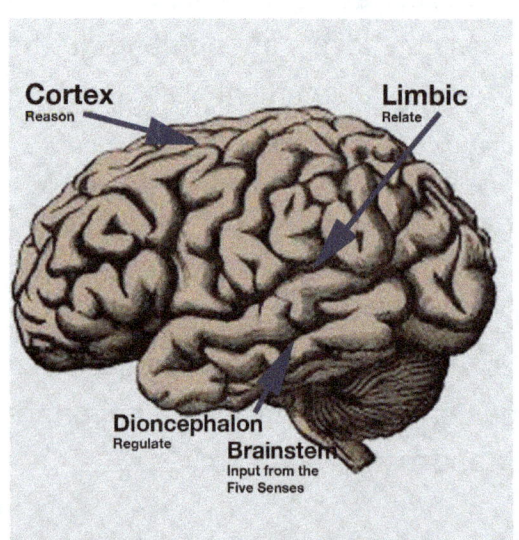

In this emotional limbic brain region, the teacher can relate to and connect with the child. Here we recommend short, soft sentences, clear boundaries, and kind words that accompany their efforts at mastery and purpose. Cultivating a sense of belonging by introducing neurotransmitters like oxytocin and serotonin has the added impact of making the child feel invited, safe and "part of" the activities at hand.

Finally, as the child is feeling safe, happy and engaged, they are able to access their higher order thinking and reasoning brain in the frontal lobes. This is the ideal time to talk to the child, or to introduce new constructs and emotions that allow them to activate the power of their thinking conscious brain. It is a place for reason and accountability, for abstract thinking, and also a place for judgment and predicting. In this executive space, the child will be able to visualize and make references to the regulating brain, the emotional brain, and even their reasoning brain (in a metacognitive way).

In this Practical Guide, we focused on the three imperatives that reflect these regions of the brain as described above. In our experience, when teachers follow this journey they can expect excellence in teaching that transcribes into brilliance in learning.

We began with **Section One: Regulate**. We have to assume with each new lesson before the children arrived in class, that they had something distressing and even stressful happen to them that caused them to be dysregulated. In the hierarchical model of a child's brain, we begin at the survival place – the diencephalon. We describe simple practicable solutions that engage at a primitive juncture and invite safety and community. The objective of these exercises is to connect the dysregulated child with their limbic emotional brain.

A dysregulated child, while transfixed in involuntary routines and negative behavior, is nevertheless building structures that are not helpful for future learning in that space. "Regulate" is all about safety — this is not the time to reason with the child who is experiencing their primitive brain. However, it is the perfect time for co-regulation - a time to build vital white matter structures for safety, attachment, and sense of belonging that are designed to be cumulatively present for the entirety of the child's future.

We cannot assume that just because children have arrived in class, that they are ready to learn. Having erred on the side of caution, we assume that all new class members need to co-regulate with us first, and then practice self-regulation. This helps them gain experience with inhibition and metacognition in readiness (and "RAS-iness") for learning. In this primal brain region, we are intentional about laying down foundational structures, by enacting routines, predictiveness, and safety - both physical and psychological.

In **Section Two: Relate,** we continue to harness the strengths of the child who is invested in a feeling of safety and security that comes from consistency, predictability and kindness. We layer in more security by reinforcing through cognitive rehearsal, the primal and emotional links to self – the brain's Me Here Now. This can be accomplished through a keen awareness of students' mindsets through detailed knowledge about each child's passions and dreams, which are made visible through interactive dialogue and story telling. We ensure that each class is psychologically safe and predictable. In such a safe space, it is easier to show vulnerability and begin to understand tolerance for ambiguity. We use non-judgmental discussions that accentuate every nuance relating to the child, and elicit moods, feelings, and energies to facilitate decentering, empathy, and mastery.

Relationship building is always more accomplished when there is ample serotonin, oxytocin, and other powerful neurotransmitters in the learning space. In addition, consistent and predictable use of long-term potentiation techniques enhances the sense of achievement through personalized idea generation, contributions to deep understanding, and engagement.

In **Section Three: Reason,** we include more ideas for engaging children who have successfully navigated to their executive function frontal lobes by engaging their higher-order processing skills. Here, we anchor our thinking in the knowledge that this part of the child's brain facilitates fluency in thinking about experiences retrieved from the past using their memory system, assembling these with events that are happening in the present, as well as predictions for occasions and plans that can happen in the future. This activates a two-way demand on working memory and long-term encoded memories, emotional connections to people, places and things, with distant core memories of safety episodes that are in the past.

As you make visible the child's level of comprehension in relation to identity, appetites, and passions, it becomes increasingly easy to introduce opportunities for bigger, more expansive and deeper analogies and metaphors. Typically, the child will reach for and cognitively stretch to places that are new, challenging, and often barely manageable.

The child will also display a new interest and growing capacity to inhibit behaviors that used to dominate, overcome hungry desires for immediate gratification, and take initial steps into managing crises that used to be beyond their control. It is exciting to play in the higher-order mental activations that can be consolidated further with neurotransmitters that include GABA, norepinephrine, and dopamine.

Dr. Bruce Perry developed this powerful emotional 3R schema - Regulate, Relate, Reason - to facilitate a re-engagement with the thinking brain when a person is stressed and operating in survival mode. Just like everything else that we know about teaching and learning - scaffolds that work for children who are hypervigilant, who are stressed, and who suffer from anxiety and low self-esteem - these same scaffolds work for all children. And they work every time - consistently, predictably, and kindly.

The emotional 3R scaffold takes the pressure off the child's working memory system - releasing the space so that the child can use it for processing new information or difficult complex constructs. In addition, these same scaffold elements alleviate the sympathetic nervous system - allowing the child to access the limbic and forebrain higher-order processing brain. Finally, this simple scaffold allows the teacher to communicate with ease to the child's brain because they have engaged first in the primal brain, then approached the emotional brain, before progressing to the sapiens sapiens brain where the modern child can excel and thrive.

Glossary

A

Active Avoidance: a behavior in which a child will avoid a negative outcome by taking a direct overt action. An example might be when a child will finish cleaning his room, or write a thank you note to a cranky aunt, in order to appease mom who had threatened to confiscate his favorite computer game or iPhone for a week.

Adverse Childhood Experiences (ACEs): children who witness traumatic events at an early age might demonstrate difficulties engaging in normal school life. Experiences are varied and include physical abuse, sexual abuse, emotional abuse, physical neglect, mental illness, incarcerated relative (especially mom or dad), and mother mistreated with violence. High ACEs predict crises in health, capacity for attachment, and educational opportunity.

Agency: a metacognitive engagement where learners take active ownership of their own learning. This contrasts with Active Avoidance, where children might acquiesce to study, so that they might avoid an aversive event or punishment.

Amygdala Hijack: an immediate, overwhelming emotional response, with a later realization that the response was inappropriately strong given the trigger. It is responsible for an involuntary freeze, fight, flight, or fawn response to the threat.

Aphasia: a brain disorder where a person has trouble speaking or understanding other people speaking. This happens with damage or disruptions in parts of the brain that control spoken language and understanding. It often happens with conditions like stroke.

Appetite over Aptitude: all children have (sometimes hidden) desires and plans. When such plans are made visible in classroom settings, a teacher might recognize the child's appetite for information and attentional arousal in relation to these items. Instead of focusing on a child's aptitude for a subject, it is more appropriate to follow the child's appetite for something that the child is passionate about and reworking that love of engagement to the child's aptitude.

Associationism: in Pavlovian conditioning, an association can be made between a physical event and a mentalistic involuntary activation. For instance, your puppy might sit and present sad eyes when it arrives back from playing frisbee so that you will respond with a favorable treat.

Asynchronous Development: all regions of the brain do not necessarily mature in sync with each other. Based on individualized circumstances, different regions of the brain grow at varying rates and at various time points (asynchronously). Therefore, children should not be compared one against the other, based on the spurious idea that because they are all aged three, they should all have the same learning capabilities.

Attachment Disorder: when social and emotional trauma is associated with a child's early years, the child may suffer from failure to bond, or become unresponsive to social interaction. This can occur when there is severe neglect of the child's physical or emotional needs (especially from the primary caregiver) and this can persist across the lifespan.

Automaticity: an automatic process that can be carried out without mental effort. Such states in learning systems are valuable because they are accompanied by a dramatic reduction in cognitive load. Such learning experiences allow the child to free up working memory so that the child can attend to more immediate needs for survival or attention.

Autonomic Nervous System (ANS) Reactivity: a measure of a child's psycho-biologic response to challenges in the environment, which is associated with physical, behavioral, and mental health symptoms. Increased ANS reactivity responses to laboratory challenges (compared with resting states) have been associated with high illness rates, internalizing and externalizing behavior problems, and mental health symptoms including anxiety, withdrawal, and overall poor adjustment in school academic activities.

Autonomy: independent self-determination where a child is acting from choice, rather than feeling pressured to act. This form of autonomy is considered a fundamental psychological need that predicts well-being.

B

Backwards Design: is a method of designing educational instruction by deciding on a Big Idea, then scaffolding that construct with two supporting constructs that connect meaningful information (relevant content) to the Big Idea. It's called backward because it starts with the end (the enduring idea) in mind and works backward from there.

Basal Ganglia: this region of the brain is heavily involved with learning systems since it consists of structures that engage in memory, emotion, voluntary motor movements, habits, eye movement, conditional learning, procedural learning, and cognition.

Behavior as Communication: in schools, behavior is typically perceived as either bad or good. But, in reality, there is a neural substrate to all behavior. When this dimension is explored, it is possible to connect all behavior with communication. In the classroom, a child who is acting up or acting out, may be communicating that the environment is ill-supportive of white matter structures that are needed for the task at hand (e.g., focusing on-task) may in fact, not be myelinated in place yet, which fact would make it nigh impossible for the child to do that task. This communication might sway the teacher's approach to building myelinated neuronal tracts for focus before requiring that a child attend to focus.

Big Idea: in backwards design, the successful facilitator will end up with a clear understanding of the Big Idea which is the central focus of the material that is being delivered or taught. Another way to understand Big Idea is to state that when people leave this classroom or meeting they will walk away with ONE enduring understanding: the Big Idea. If the facilitator does not have an understanding of the Big Idea, then students will probably have no corresponding comprehension of the Big Idea either.

Boredom: a child that is experiencing boredom may portray a limited attention span and lack of interest in what's happening in the learning space. They may also feel apathetic, fatigued, nervous, or jittery. In some cases, boredom can make it more challenging to focus and cause a learner to feel stressed or distracted. Neurologists report that areas in the brain that light up for a child claiming to be bored, are the same areas that light up when a child is stressed.

Bounce Balls: effective way to increase blood flow to a child's brain, increase focus, and enhance neurotransmitter production for optimal learning.

Brain-Derived Neurotrophic Factor (BDNF): a crucial protein that is essential for maintaining healthy neurons and creating new neurons. BDNF is essential to learning because it is related to plasticity in the brain and enhanced memory. Physical exercise is linked to BDNF production.

Broca's Area: a region in the frontal lobe of the left hemisphere with functions linked to speech production. Language processing has been linked to this part of the brain—Broca's area—since Pierre Paul Broca examined impairments in several patients who suffered from aphasia in the 1860s.

C

Cerebellum: Latin for "Little Brain," this brain structure is located where the spinal cord meets the brain. It contains more than half of the brain's neurons and specialized cells that transmit information via electrical signals. It receives information from sensory systems such as touch, sound, smell, the spinal cord and other parts of the brain, and regulates motor movements, walking, running, lifting.

Child-centric: teaching with a focus on the child, as opposed to content or high stakes testing. In such a methodology, teachers are more interested in architecting a child's brain, than in filling the brain with information that can be regurgitated in tests later.

Choice: allowing children to make a decision, or series of decisions, with materials and content in learning systems so that they can make mistakes in a safe scaffolded environment and subsequently learn to make more informed decisions in the future.

Chunking: mindful of Miller's Law, teachers deliver information in small chunks, so children who are still growing their working memory capacity can access the big ideas.

Circuits: a population of neurons interconnected by synapses that carry out a specific function when activated. Learners grow neuronal circuitry specific to riding a bicycle or playing a particular move in soccer, by receiving mediated opportunities to practice with intention.

Clean Slate: a belief that a human infant is born with no built-in mental content and that human knowledge comes from experience and perception. This has been shown to be inaccurate, even though many people still refer to a "tabula rasa" as an example of nothing in there.

Co-regulation: the process of regulating together so a child can learn to self-regulate. Before a child has the structures in place to manage and understand their own behavior, it is usually necessary for an adult to help by "making visible" the steps needed and giving the child opportunities to make mistakes as they experiment with the process.

Cognition: includes all conscious and unconscious processes by which knowledge is accumulated, such as perceiving, recognizing, conceiving, and reasoning. Cognition involves attending to something of interest, short- and long-term memory formation and retrieval, making logical conclusions through rational thought, and by using auditory and visual processing.

Cognitive Delay: learning disabilities that can result from a wide array of circumstances, which might leave a child with difficulties in focus, learning, articulating, limitations in mental functioning, and inability to connect for social interaction. Interventions that are based on an understanding of neural plasticity can assist any child overcome cognitive delays.

Cognitive Load: the amount of resources used up by the working memory. Since working memory has been shown (Miller's Law) to have serious limitations, it makes sense that teachers should try to reduce the load that extraneous material might impact on learners' existing capacity. A simple example of cognitive load is when you are trying to attend to two conversations at the same time. Children who are convinced (erroneously) that they are multitaskers, are often hampered by the fact that they cannot attend to a gaming device and do homework at the same time.

Cognitive Model: an intentional active method of learning that optimizes the mind and maximizes the brain's potential. This model makes it easy for learners to connect prior knowledge with incoming sensory information and personalizes that new knowledge for deeper understanding that is encoded into long-term memory.

Cognitive Rehearsal: refers to a whole brain practice which involves learners ascribing attentional focus to new information. This is often achieved with scaffolding questions that include individualized reflection, revised thinking with peers in small group collaborative discussions, and report out as a group to a wider audience where feedback and discussions are welcomed.

Compliance: a child who is compliant is easy to manage, follows instructions, listens attentively if there is a danger of being punished for not being attentive, inhibits disruptive behavior to avoid teacher's ire, makes choices that are in keeping with classroom norms, and stays below the radar of the teacher.

Concentration: ability to focus one's attention on a particular task or activity. Children learn to concentrate by inhibiting distractions, single tasking, using easy to manage time scaffolds, by taking breaks as needed, and getting enough sleep.

Concrete Steps: according to Piaget, the concrete operational stage depicts an important developmental step in a child's life. When children experience difficulty absorbing and understanding new information or difficult constructs, it is acceptable to introduce a scaffold that is rooted in this concrete stage of developmental psychology. An example might be to use fingers or toes to count to ten. Teachers have discovered that all children benefit from time spent in the concrete stage, even when they are able to advance quickly and engage easily. This revert to concrete appears to ease the cognitive load and free up working memory.

Consistent Caring Adults: a concept that illustrates how positive relationships with adults can improve a child's ability to learn. The currency for systemic change is trust, and trust comes from forming healthy working relationships. People, not programs, change people. With these words, Bruce Perry calls for four consistent caring adults in every child's life.

As educators, we need to assist the child in identifying these four caring adults so that relationships are stable and lasting.

Consolidate: sleep benefits the retention of memory. Sleep as a state of greatly reduced external information processing, represents an optimal time for consolidating memories. Theories characterize sleep as a brain state optimizing memory consolidation, in opposition to the waking brain being optimized for encoding of memories. Consolidation originates from reactivation of recently encoded neuronal memory representations, which occur during slow wave sleep (SWS) and transform respective representations for integration into long-term memory. Rapid Eye Movement (REM) sleep may stabilize transformed memories.

Content-centric: when the focus of instruction is on "covering" content topics, at the expense of the child's capacity to either keep up with the scope and sequence, or processing power to manage new constructs, pacing, and breadth of issues.

Continuum: a continuous sequence in which the nearby adjacent elements differ just a little from each other, but there are large differences between the two extremes. An example might be the difference between the seasons Spring, Summer, Fall, and Winter.

Corpus Callosum: an essential structure for integration of information between the left and right cerebral hemispheres. Each hemisphere controls movement on the opposite side of the body. The corpus callosum is the largest white matter structure in the brain, consisting of 200–250 million contralateral axons that connect the hemispheres.

Cortisol: is your body's primary stress hormone, in preparation for a flight or fight situation. Cortisol is released by the adrenal glands when you are stressed or perceive danger and causes the body to react accordingly; increased heart rate, increased breathing rate, increased blood pressure, reduced digestive system, tunnel vision, and sweaty palms.

Cramming: last minute studying in an effort to stuff as much information as possible into short-term memory before a test. Typically, this exercise is accompanied by stress, anxiety and loss of sleep, with a resultant outcome that fails to meet the objective.

Cultural Norms: attitudes and behaviors that are typical for a social group with beliefs and values that are shared. These are learned and transmitted by what people think, say and do.

D

Dandelinic: a measure of autonomic nervous system reactivity (ANS) that equates with resilience. In the same way that dandelions can survive in a crack in the concrete, some individuals are endowed with enough resilience that they can overcome adverse experiences and high stress with ease.

De-escalate: to reduce the intensity of a stressful encounter, violent reaction or impending conflict. In conflict resolution, actions that are taken to lessen the potential of violence or other reactive behavior that could cause harm to others. Escalation is usually accompanied by increased levels of cortisol, so any attempt to de-escalate should involve reducing cortisol and increasing oxytocin. Useful strategies for de-escalating children in learning spaces where escalation can be very contagious and spread to others who are anxious, involve mirror neurons, breathing, listening, empathy and physical activity.

Decentering: a process of stepping outside of one's own mental events leading to an objective and non-judging stance towards the self. An example might be when a child, who's favorite pastime is riding a bicycle, is able to accept that other children may have different favorite pastimes and hobbies.

Dendritic Spines: small projections on dendrites that increase receptive properties and isolate signal specificity.

Developmental Growth: based on Piaget's theory of child development, children typically progress through the following learning stages in their journey to maturity: Sensorimotor (Birth to 2 Years); Preoperational (2 to 7 Years); Concrete Operational (7 to 11); Formal Operational (12 and up). As children engage in their environments, they carry out trial and error experiments in which they begin to make sense of their world and come to understand reality.

Diencephalon: from the Greek meaning "between-brain", the diencephalon is the area of the brain between the telencephalon (in the front) and brainstem (in the back). It consists of the Thalamus (the body's information relay station since most sensory information - with the exception of smell - that proceeds to the cortex, first stops in the thalamus before being sent on to its destination), the Subthalamus (connected with the basal ganglia, which influences motor control, motor learning, executive functions and behaviors, and emotions), the Hypothalamus (maintains homeostasis by regulating hormone secretion via the Pituitary), and the Epithalamus (with the Pineal Gland and Habenula regulates melatonin and a child's circadian rhythm). While it is not part of the lower brain, it is just above the brainstem and is important in terms of regulating mood, memory and emotions in your classroom.

Differential Neurobiological Susceptibility to Social Context: from a neuroscientific viewpoint, children are hardwired differently from birth to show up in any social context, based on their autonomic nervous system reactivity and their lived experience. Some children are born, and are predisposed to be sensitive and even ultra-sensitive in social contexts. While other children are predisposed to be resilient and capable of surviving stressful experiences.

Discipline Policies: typically, school discipline policies are designed to address student behavior so that disruptive and aggressive encounters are eliminated. In theory, this is supposed to preserve the integrity of the teaching environment so that all students can learn. In reality, progressive punitive practices (losing privileges, time out, in-school suspension, losing recess, out-of-school suspension, and expulsion) propagate stressful learning environments where hypervigilant children fail to connect.

Disequilibrium: a moment of disequilibrium causes instability in thinking systems, which demands closure by modifying existing schemata or creating whole new schemas. An example of disequilibrium might be when a child discovers that the moon and the sun are both visible in the sky during the daytime. This interferes with the notion that the moon comes out by night and the sun by day. The child will struggle to make sense of this new information that has perturbed their prior knowledge that compartmentalized day and night.

Dopamine: a very powerful neurotransmitter that is intimately linked to learning. It is closely associated with reward-motivated behavior and motor control. In a complex chemical interaction that involves molecular excitatory or inhibitory processes at the synapse, dopamine can be responsible for synaptic plasticity, which is necessary for learning and memory formation. In the classroom, teachers can increase dopamine naturally for immediate impact on mood and motivation. A healthy diet, good sleep, and lots of physical exercise are habits that can be easily introduced to your learning environment, as well as spending time outside, eliminating stress, and having fun during lessons.

Dyscalculia: a math learning disability that impairs a child's ability to learn number-related concepts, perform accurate math calculations, reason and problem solve, and perform other basic math skills. Dyscalculia may cause children to lose track of counting, not progress in mathematical concepts as quickly as peers, and may become easily frustrated with numbers. Some children with dyscalculia are fast problem solvers and are good at thinking in novel and innovative ways.

Dysfunction: an impairment in cognitive skills or motor skills that will result in the child falling behind and failing to meet potential.

Dysgraphia: a neurological disorder characterized by writing disabilities. Specifically, the disorder causes a person's writing to be distorted or incorrect. Typically a child might display difficulties writing with a pencil, writing in a straight line, writing letters backwards or not remembering what letters look like. Appropriate treatments can be provided by experts who can assess the child's small motor, memory or other neural/cognitive skills.

Dyslexia: a learning disorder that involves difficulty with decoding verbal interactions. When children have difficulties identifying speech sounds and learning how they relate to letters and words. While Dyslexia can delay fluency, there are hands-on scaffolds that can help a child overcome this delay. Experts can teach decoding skills using multi-sensory approaches and tailor whole brain methods to suit the child.

E

Ebbinghaus Forgetting Curve: a concept developed by German psychologist Hermann Ebbinghaus. He discovered that over time, people were unable to retain the new information that they learned. He was able to reliably demonstrate a decline in memory that was consistent with time elapsed. Such a scientific model holds true when information is presented in a traditional "terminal objective" methodology that guarantees that all topics are "covered." At the same time, when a cognitive approach is used and the focus of the class becomes not content or topics but learners, memory becomes a learning tool in the co-created process.

Empathy: the ability to comprehend and share the feelings of others, by imagining ourselves in their experiences. In the classroom, children begin to cognitively understand another child's point of view and accept that it is a valid option. Similarly, a child might be able to feel the happiness or pain of another person and understand that it is something that can be shared. From a cognitive and neural architecture standpoint, children need to play and practice in the emotional limbic parts of their brains, so that they can build white matter structures for empathy, tolerance for ambiguity, and social interaction.

Epigenetic: how your behaviors and environment can cause changes that affect the way your genes work. Unlike genetic changes, epigenetic changes are reversible and do not change your DNA sequence, but they can change how your body reads a DNA sequence. In other words, the environment is a causal link to how your genes turn on or off. In school settings, the environment is something that you have control over and therefore can be a powerful influence on a child's behavior.

Episodic Memory: the time something happened together with the details of recent or past experiences. Episodic differs from semantic memory which is about describing what something is, and they both make up declarative memories. An example of an episodic memory might be who was with you at this year's Thanksgiving Dinner and what you ate.

Executive Function: mental processes that enable one to plan, focus attention, remember instructions, and juggle multiple tasks successfully. The brain needs this skillset to filter distractions, prioritize tasks, set and achieve goals, and control impulses. The executive function is located in the frontal lobes of the brain, where structures are connected from the cerebellum and the other lobes - occipital, temporal, and parietal.

Expected Behavior: behavior that is age and developmental appropriate. In school settings, children are often punished for behavior that is deemed "unexpected" based on arbitrary rules that have been put in place by individuals who are tasked with maintaining standards for the school system. Very often, these rules and expected norms have not been co-created with the children who are, in fact, the principal stakeholders and long-term beneficiaries. Many behaviors that have been drawn up by adults, are exactly the behaviors that are not appropriate for the developmental age of the children that are being punished.

Extrinsic Motivation: behavior is motivated by an external factor influencing a person to do an activity in hopes of earning a reward – or avoiding a punishment. Stemming from a behaviorist framework, extrinsic motivation has been shown to be less effective than intrinsic motivation when there is even a modicum of cognitive load involved.

F

Fasciculus: a bundle of nerve fibers or wires that conduct electro-chemical information in neural networks. In the human brain, several major and minor fasciculi represent bundles of axons that connect different regions of the brain. For instance, the Superior Longitudinal Fasciculus connects the back of the brain with the front of the brain, and in effect links the frontal, temporal and parietal with the occipital lobe. Similarly, the Arcuate Fasciculus connects Broca's and Wernicke's areas for the production and understanding of language.

Filter: approximately 11 million bits of information comes into your brain every second, but your conscious brain can only handle roughly 40 bits per second. Luckily, we have a dedicated clump of neurons called the Reticular Activating System (RAS) that acts as the brain's filter to manage what is filtered out so that your brain is not overwhelmed. A simple example of how the RAS filter works might be how a mom can hear her baby call out even when she is in a noisy room filled with lots of other sounds. The filter blocks out the extraneous sounds and allows her baby's call to stand out. Similarly, when you learn a new vocabulary word, the RAS filter will find it everywhere. In school, a child's RAS filter might confirm the belief that "I am no good at math" and misinterpret a teacher's kind attempts at giving feedback, as confirming that indeed my inner voice (RAS filter) was correct (I am no good at math).

Freeze, Fight, Flight or Fawn: these four "Fs" are automatic involuntary behaviors that accompany stress, fear, anxiety and other situations that crop up in classrooms where children are learning to co-regulate. Freeze is your body's inability to move or act against a threat. The Fight response is your body's way of facing any perceived threat aggressively. Flight means your body urges you to run from danger. Fawn is your body's stress response to try to please someone to avoid conflict.

Frontal Lobes: the front part of the brain that is responsible for higher order processing and cognitive functions that make us who we are. When a child is engaged in learning activities, it is ideal if the child is able to access the frontal lobes. It is here that they will be able to carry out functions like memory encoding and retrieval, expressing and controlling emotions, playing, predicting, metacognitive impulse control, problem solving, reasoning and rational thought, social interaction, and motor function.

G

GABA: an amino acid that functions as the primary inhibitory neurotransmitter for the central nervous system (CNS). Gamma-aminobutyric acid (GABA) functions to reduce neuronal excitability by inhibiting nerve transmission. GABA is known for producing a calming effect. It's thought to play a major role in controlling nerve cell hyperactivity associated with anxiety, stress and fear.

Gene Expression: Gene expression is a tightly regulated process that allows a cell to respond to its changing environment. It acts as both an on/off switch to control when proteins are made, and also a volume control that increases or decreases the amount of proteins made. Social context is a vital element in whether genes are turned on or off. For this reason, children's early life experiences can have major influence and consequences for their ability to learn in social contexts.

Genotype: a person's unique sequence of DNA. More specifically, genotype is used to refer to the two alleles a person has inherited for a particular gene. For instance, a child might inherit a short expression of the serotonin transporter gene from the biological mom and a short expression of the serotonin transporter gene from the biological dad, resulting in a short short genotype.

Goal-Directed: behavior driven by an expectation that it is likely to bring about a desired outcome. Goal-directed decisions leverage causal knowledge of the potential consequences of actions in order to flexibly pursue a current goal. Children start to grow and learn about their surroundings by their instincts. Over time and with practice, they start to participate in deliberate, goal-directed behaviors. During goal-directed behavior, children begin to think about what they want to do, how and where to achieve it, and then they perform an action to do it.

Growth Mindset: describes the underlying beliefs children have about learning and intelligence. In a growth mindset, children believe that their most basic abilities can be developed through dedication and hard work—brains and talent are just the starting point. This view creates a love of learning and a resilience that is essential for great accomplishment.

H

Habituate: a decrease of a response to a repeated eliciting stimulus that is not due to sensory adaptation or motor fatigue. Essentially, the individual learns to stop responding to a stimulus, which is no longer biologically relevant. The habituation process is a form of adaptive behavior (neuroplasticity) that is classified as non-associative learning. For example, people may habituate to repeated sudden loud noises when they learn these have no consequences. An example in learning spaces might be that over time, the sound of a jet taking off from the nearby airport stops interfering with the children's attention.

Hardwired: in the child's brain, electrical circuits in which the connections among components are permanently established. These circuits are designed to perform specific functions. While neural plasticity is a central tenet of teaching and learning, some circuits are already in place and will be activated involuntarily when triggered. For instance, even if there is a rule that we shouldn't scream when we are surprised, a loud scary noise might cause some children to scream uncontrollably.

Hebb's Rule: a neuro-scientific theory claiming that an increase in synaptic efficacy arises from a presynaptic cell's repeated and persistent stimulation of a postsynaptic cell. It is an attempt to explain synaptic plasticity, the adaptation of brain neurons during the learning process. Neurons that fire together, wire together. Donald Hebb was a neurophysiologist who contributed to learning sciences by establishing the causal link between neural substrates and behavior.

Higher Cognitive Functions: a set of cognitive processes – including attentional control, inhibitory control, working memory, and cognitive flexibility, as well as reasoning, problem solving, and planning – that are necessary for the cognitive control of behavior (selecting and successfully monitoring behaviors that facilitate the attainment of chosen goals). Executive functions mature at different rates over time. Some abilities peak maturation rate in late childhood or adolescence, while others' progress into early adulthood. The brain continues to mature and develop connections well into adulthood. A person's executive function abilities are shaped by both physical changes in the brain, and by life experiences in the classroom and outside.

Hippocampus: shaped like a seahorse, this complex neural structure is situated deep in the temporal lobe and is connected to the amygdala and other important structures that make it a center of emotion, learning, memory, and the autonomic nervous system. Being an integral part of the emotional limbic system, a child's hippocampus plays a vital role in regulating learning, memory encoding, memory consolidation, and spatial navigation.

Hypersensitive: when a child is overly sensitive to things like smells, sounds, tastes, or textures. This shows up in classrooms if certain triggers cause children to become reactive, disruptive and aggressive. Teachers may have children who show poor ability to focus due to constant noise and distraction.

I

Implicit Memory: Information that you remember unconsciously and effortlessly. Implicit memory is unconscious automatic memory that does not require conscious recollection of past events or information, and the individual is unaware that remembering has occurred.

Imposter Syndrome: feelings of self-doubt and personal incompetence that persist despite education, experience, and accomplishments. To counter these feelings, a child might end up working harder and holding themselves to ever higher standards.

Inhibit: a cognitive process that permits a child to inhibit their impulses and natural, habitual, or dominant behavioral responses to stimuli. Executive functions in the prefrontal cortex play a critical role in the regulation of emotion and behavior by anticipating the consequences of actions and inhibiting behaviors. Teachers create scenarios that give children opportunities to play in this inhibition space, so that they can make mistakes in a safe learning environment.

Innate Capacity: ability skills and traits that are present from birth. Children have the innate ability to speak, whereas animals do not.

Intentionality: empowers the prediction and explanation of human behavior based on beliefs and desires. In school settings, teachers with mental models that include neural plasticity can be intentional about building neural structures that facilitate reading, writing, or mathematics.

Intrinsic Motivation: the act of doing something without any obvious external rewards. You do it because it's enjoyable and interesting, rather than because of an outside incentive or pressure to do it, such as a reward or deadline. In learning spaces, teachers create intrinsic motivation by facilitating lessons so that children experience autonomy, mastery and purpose.

Involuntary Reaction: breathing, digestion, heart beating, eye reflexes are examples of involuntary activations. Other involuntary reactions can occur when the brain is hardwired to react to danger, surprise, or novelty. An involuntary reaction will occur when a child reacts to immediate danger such as accidentally touching a hot object.

J

Jealousy (as motivation): an emotion children experience when there's a real or perceived threat to a relationship. However, like most emotions, jealousy (or envy) can be both helpful and unhelpful. It can motivate children to better themselves and achieve success. It can highlight things they want but don't yet have, and when they know what they want, they're in a far better position to work towards it.

Judgmental: if children have an excessively critical point of view because they form opinions of people and situations very quickly; it might be better for them to wait until they know more about the person or situation.

K

Kind: teachers who are typically caring, generous, warm and friendly, are able to build relationships with children who are often on the lookout (hypervigilant) for danger, stress, mistrust. Other qualities that foster good relationship-building include amiability, compassionate, courteous, cordial, and considerate.

Knee Jerk (response): an automatic or instinctive reaction that occurs when a child reacts to an event or person in an unthinking way. An example of a knee jerk reaction in a school setting might be when a child physically and hurtfully pushes a peer away until they realize they were about to give them a surprise gift.

L

Labeling: to label is to limit. Labeling a child limits our understanding of who they are. Once you label a child, we lose the child's complexities, and it is in the complexities where we find the true self with all its uniqueness. Labeling others can actually limit what you see in them. We need to look beyond labels to find the true self.

Lagging: some children underperform at school. This can occur for reasons that are grounded in medical problems, brain injury, learning disabilities, attention deficits, emotional problems, poor socio-cultural home environment, psychiatric disorders, and even environmental causes. In many cases, children are able to catch up with support from specialists in the classroom, or in sessions outside of class.

Limbic: a complex set of brain structures located on both sides of the thalamus. The limbic system supports a variety of functions including emotion, behavior, motivation, long-term memory, and olfaction. Emotional life is largely housed in the limbic system, and it has a great deal to do with the formation of memories. The limbic area controls basic emotions (fear, pleasure, anger) and drives (hunger, sex, dominance, care of offspring).

Long-Term Memory: information can be stored for long periods of time. While short-term and working memory persist for only about 18 to 30 seconds, information can remain in long-term memory indefinitely. The hippocampus and sleep are important factors for encoding into long term. The memories are rearranged and stored in regions of the neocortex that are appropriate for the kind of information involved.

Long-Term Potentiation (LTP): a strengthening of synaptic connections between two neurons that are activated simultaneously. Pertains to memory and learning. In the classroom, there are specific activities that support Long-Term Potentiation.

M

Malleable: the ability to change, shift, and flex. Neural plasticity is sometimes referred to as a malleable brain. This kind of plasticity is a central precept about learning – the brain is able to rewire itself. This is one of the amazingly complex elements about a child's brain; an ability to change, reorganize and grow networks that allow the child to advance and mature. Incoming sensory information causes physical changes at a molecular level so that a child is able to perceive, understand, and do new things. Children are more malleable than adults. In theory, if educational systems were set up correctly, children should excel in schools.

Mastery: comprehensive knowledge of a skill or subject. All children can achieve a level of mastery in any subject matter, if given time and attention with a predictable, consistent, and kind teacher in a system that follows that same principle. In other words, eliminate labeling, stratification, rewards and punishments and expect competence. When a child achieves mastery in skills and concepts, it is accompanied with appropriate levels of neurotransmitters that promote more learning and new opportunities for accessing deeper and broader challenges.

Me Here Now: when a child can relate an idea to themselves, in that place, and in that time. The human brain is highly focused on anything that affects the individual personally, in the moment and space. From that point of view, it makes some sense to try to associate any new information to a child's personal experience, so that they can see the relevance and salience of the incoming sensory information and associate it with prior knowledge that is also personal and meaningful at a primal level.

Memory: bits of information that are stored for later retrieval so that we can engage in the world around us. We learn from past experiences and assimilate that knowledge with anticipated upcoming events, people and places, so that we can make decisions that are of particular interest to us. Although memory is unstable, fickle, transient and unreliable, it helps make us who we are. Without memory our lives would be highly impoverished.

Mental Model: representation of concepts, frameworks, or worldviews that you carry around in your mind. Mental models are thinking tools that one uses to understand life, make decisions, and solve problems. They can derive from a belief structure that helps us explain how the world works. A teacher with a mental model that the child's working memory is no bigger than a pinhead, will approach information management in a very different way to the teacher who has no mental model about limitations of working memory.

Metacognitive: thinking about one's thinking. Knowledge about one's own information processing and strategies that influence one's learning that can optimize future learning. A child who is able to think about their own thinking, is doing so with structures that connect the cerebellum with the four other lobes. This is an important higher-order executive process that builds a powerful architecture in the brain.

Miller's Law: a 1956 paper entitled, *The Magical Number Seven Plus or Minus Two*; according to George Miller, memory span is not limited in terms of bits, but rather, in terms of chunks. His research defined the limitation of human working memory to roughly seven new concepts at any one sitting. Nelson Cowan, revisiting Miller's research in 2001, offered a newer and updated limitation to working memory (Three or Four Plus or Minus Two).

Mindset: according to the work of Carol Dweck, children can have a fixed or a growth mindset in relation to their understanding of the constructs, intelligence and talent. Children who are convinced that other people have more intelligence than them, work from a place of deficit – a fixed mindset. Children who believe that intelligence, like talent, is malleable, come with a different perspective: a growth mindset. Children who have a growth mindset believe they can develop their talents and improve over time. When students have a growth mindset, they typically have a passion for learning.

Mirror Neurons: a group of neurons that activate when we perform an action or when we see an action being performed. Mirror neurons are essential for imitation - a key factor in the learning process. Children do have mirror neurons and they can be cultivated and enhanced so that children can experience and practice empathy, de-escalation, and learn from peers. With appropriate co-regulation from the teacher, children can feel empathy and then subsequently show empathy.

Misconceptions: misconceptions commonly result from personal experience and interactions with the physical world. In the social sciences, they are more likely derived from social sources, such as social interactions or media misinterpretation. Children's "received opinion" is commonly attributed to social media like Facebook, Twitter and Instagram, where shallow exploration allows quick easy conclusions to accumulate and consolidate.

Mistakes: excellent learning opportunities. Learning from failure is often the key to success. By getting things wrong, children improve their skills and grow in various ways. When students are mindful of incorrect solution concepts while working on a problem, they are able to deal with the problem at a much deeper level, than someone who is just presented with the correct solution and has to memorize it.

Myelination: a fatty sheath wrapped around nerve fibers. Through its special construction, myelin accelerates the propagation of impulses along nerve fibers. Myelin is an essential part of white matter. The main purpose of a myelin sheath is to increase the speed at which impulses propagate along the myelinated fiber. Along unmyelinated fibers, impulses move continuously as waves but, in myelinated fibers, they "hop" or propagate by saltatory conduction. Teachers can help children myelinate by providing opportunities for cognitive rehearsal in whole brain teaching methods - use the cerebellum and all four lobes.

N

Negative Mindset: patterns that make children slip from feeling positive and capable of getting results, into a negative fog that makes them feel all actions are pointless and doomed to failure. Downward negative spirals typically start with a negative thought. Such thinking reinforces and is predicated from priming in the reticular activating system (RAS) that can be changed. Teach RAS to children so that they are able to understand and eliminate their negative mindsets.

Negative Spiral: catastrophic thinking in a series of negative thoughts can feel overwhelming. Once a child gets in a negative headspace because of the first thought, it's easier to anxiously think of more negative thoughts. This negative anxiety spiral may leave the child overthinking and running through worst-case scenarios.

Neocortex: two large cerebral hemispheres that play a dominant role in human cognition. These hemispheres have been responsible for the development of language, abstract thought, imagination, and consciousness. Flexible and with infinite learning abilities, the neocortex has enabled the development of human culture.

Neural Diverse: children's brains, like all brains, are unique and different. Through a neural diversity-based mindset, teachers can more effectively address a wide range of learning needs, and prepare all students for life beyond school.

Neural Lens: neural educators view teaching and learning as collaborative, co-constructed practices that grow cognitive capacity with the goal of helping every student reach their full potential. Classrooms are viewed as greenhouses that promote neural growth.

Neural Substrate: a term used in neuroscience to indicate the part of the central nervous system (i.e., brain and spinal cord) that underlies a specific behavior, cognitive process, or psychological state. In the classroom, the teacher is looking for a neural solution to behaviors that spring from cognitive load, impaired cognitive processing, or limitations to working memory.

Neurobiological: hardwired. Cells of the nervous system play a role in the regulation of human behavior and processing of various information. Children are hardwired learning machines. Naturally and innately they seek solutions, closure to questions that are meaningful to them and are programmed to find joy, fulfillment and sense of belonging in learning and teaching environments.

Neuroplasticity: ability of the brain to change in response to environmental influences. Teachers can control the learning environment and students can thrive in an environment that is designed to provide a sense of belonging, in predictable, consistent, and kind ways.

Neurotransmitter: a chemical released by neurons to transmit an electrical signal chemically between one neuron to the next, in order to pass on a signal to and from the central nervous system. For instance, the neurotransmitter dopamine is packaged into a synaptic vesicle and stored until action potentials induce the release of dopamine into the synaptic cleft and cause binding to dopamine receptors on the postsynaptic neuron.

Norepinephrine: a neurotransmitter that increases alertness, arousal and attention. When the teacher is intentional about cultivating classroom activities that elicit norepinephrine, the children will be more inclined towards engagement and agency.

O

Occipital Lobe: the rearmost lobe in each cerebral hemisphere of the cerebral cortex. The occipital lobe is the visual processing center of the human brain. In whole brain teaching, the children are expressly given opportunities to play in the occipital lobe. For instance, they can perform some tasks behind their backs, blindfolded, with one eye shut and so on, so that the visual processing is sharpened in relation to the activity in hand.

Olfactory System: a neural structure of the vertebrate forebrain involved in the sense of smell. In whole brain teaching and learning, the children are given opportunities to engage in the work through the sense of smell for deep understanding and alternative processing.

Orchidial: in contrast to dandelinic (resilient) children who thrive in any environment, orchidial children tend to be more sensitive and need a supportive environment to learn. When the teacher focuses attention on the sensitivity of children in the classroom, there is an increased chance that all children will feel a sense of belonging, develop a growth mindset notion of their abilities and engage in a generative and contributory way to the learning space.

Oxytocin: a key neurotransmitter needed to build trust-based relationships. The teacher who is adept at filling the learning space with oxytocin (through stories, music, dance and so on) will experience a much easier path to relationship building, trust and sense of belonging.

P

Paradigm Shift: a way of looking at the world. In learning sciences, teachers are familiar with a Skinnerian paradigm, where children are rewarded for doing something that is judged compliant behavior and punished for doing something that is not in compliance with accepted behavior. A cognitive paradigm introduces teachers to a paradigm that is focused on architecting a child's brain, rather than filling a child's brain with knowledge that needs to be regurgitated for tests later.

Parietal Lobe: a region of the human brain that is important for motor, integration of information from other regions and for learning. This region also receives and processes sensory information that pertains to taste, temperature, and touch.

Perseverance: effort and practice to stick with tasks, goals, and passions. In school, Perseverance is an indicator of a growth mindset and often tops aptitude and raw talent as a more accurate predictor of achievement.

Personalized Learning: a co-created learning space where teachers, students and other stakeholders, plan lessons that take into account the child's needs, capacity, and motivation. Children experience more choice, more opportunities for mastery, and can link their learning with their purpose and passions. This kind of a learning space can lead to more motivated children who are engaged and take responsibility for their own learning.

Phenotype: interaction between genotype and environment will result in an observable trait (e.g., eye color) - expressions of genes that make the person who they are. The environment will have a large impact on how the child shows up in the world.

Phonological Loop: plays a key role in vocabulary acquisition. A clear awareness of, and ability to work with, sounds in spoken language setting the stage for decoding, blending, and ultimately, word reading. Phonological awareness begins developing before the beginning of formal schooling and continues through third grade and beyond. The phonological loop is to help children learn language and expand their vocabulary. It keeps track of new unfamiliar words while they are being added to the long-term internal word dictionary.

Predictable: easy to anticipate actions or anticipate what comes next. In schools, children often feel anxious because they may not know what is coming next, if the teacher will be upset or angry. An example of predictability is the teacher welcoming the children at the classroom door every morning, just as predictable as the sun rising every morning.

Preparation for Future Learning (PFL): instead of asking children to memorize information and regurgitate it back for a high-stakes test, modern learning systems are more interested in preparing the children's brains for future learning. It is widely agreed that the requirements for work and life in the next fifty years will possibly be even more challenging and demanding, and a preparation for adapting to these kinds of situations will require a more versatile and flexible brain.

Prior Knowledge: knowledge the learner already has before they gain new information. The teacher typically tries to make explicit a child's prior knowledge, so that the child is able to make sense of the new information by comparison and contrast.

Progressive Punitive Practice: incremental interventions to address behaviors that are deemed inappropriate in schools, with the ultimate goal of teaching prosocial behavior. Progressive discipline seeks concurrent accountability and behavior change. Problems with progressive punitive practice are widespread, since these practices rarely take the child's autonomic nervous system reactivity into account, or cultural and social constructs that introduce stressors for the child.

Public Shaming: use of electronic gadgets, clipping, or other visible formats to correct a child's behavior or point out faults. Colorful electronic methods can lead to damaging outcomes for a child—public displays that should not be done at all. Public shaming is harmful. Whilst it might be intended to reduce undesired behaviors, the recipient of public shame suffers a loss of reputation, self-esteem, and sense of belonging to the community. These effects are long-lasting and usually disproportionate to the act.

Q

Questions in a Cognitive Model: anyone, anyone! When we "teach to the orchid" child, we shy away from asking direct questions to a group of children. Questions are okay, in the right setting at the right moment. However, public shaming that always results from competitive questioning and fishing for the "right" answer, usually comes up with the exact opposite outcome. In a neural pedagogic model, three scaffolding questions are impactful for inviting all learners into the co-created space, and in particular, for achieving agency and critical thinking.

R

RAS (Reticular Activating System): a bundle of nerves in the brainstem that filters out unnecessary sensory inputs so the important information gets through. Since roughly eleven million bits of information enters the brain every second, this RAS acts like a filter and allows the most important (according to your priming) information through to your conscious mind. The RAS is the reason you learn a new word and then start hearing it everywhere. In the classroom, a child who believes that he or she is no good at math will trigger the RAS to confirm this belief all day. Thus, when the teacher focuses on the math problems that were incorrect, this information, instead of being useful corrective information, is interpreted by the RAS as confirming that, in fact, they are no good at math.

Reminders: verbal prompts to keep the student focused and on track, designed to build habits over time. In theory, reminders should be useful in class, but they often backfire to result in doing more damage than good. An occasional reminder might be effective at times. However, as most teachers will attest, we spend inordinate amounts of time reminding the same kids day after day. Typically, the reminder elicits the exact opposite effect than was anticipated – the child is publicly shamed and goes into a survival reactive mode. The reminder fails to reach the child's executive center and all the other children associate the public shaming with the affected child who is isolated and othered.

Resilience: the ability to withstand, address, adapt and adjust to misfortunes, overcome obstacles, and to bounce back from perceived failure, disappointment, or rejection. How a student learns to handle hurdles can have a lasting impact on future careers and relationships.

Revert to Default: while many people welcome change, it is easy to forget about the inevitable implementation dip, where outcomes fail to achieve the anticipated levels of success that was promised. In fact, things can look very much worse in the early hours, days and weeks following the change. It is in this phase of lost productivity and dwindling confidence that people tend to revert to default, abandon the new effort and return to the "old" tried and true way of doing business.

S

Saltatory Conduction: the way an electrical impulse jumps from node to node along an axon. Like pebbles bouncing along the bed of a fast moving stream, an electric charge will bounce (saltate) from node to node down the axonal fiber to the terminal. Similarly, an action potential jumps from node to node, in a process called saltatory conduction, which can increase conduction velocity up to ten times, without an increase in axonal diameter. Myelinated axons can conduct an electric current at velocities up to 150 m/s.

Scaffolding Questions: three questions of a pedagogic model that are brain-based and designed to elicit critical thinking. Each question is associated with an exercise that causes the brain to engage at the appropriate level. For instance, the question dealing with surprise is designed to free the brain from a reactive survival stance (is it safe here, am I ok?), by prompting the child to think about something emotional that is associated with the topic at hand.

Schemas: cognitive frameworks that help us to organize and interpret information. They are developed through experience and can affect cognitive processing. Piaget viewed schemas as basic blocks of intelligent behavior. In the classroom, children will develop schemas that reflect the practice and routines that teachers present. Some children may develop schemas that hinder their ability to learn (such as learned helplessness).

Self-regulation: the ability to self-manage impulses and inhibit thoughts that land the child in trouble. A child will develop self-awareness so they can consciously recognize their thoughts, feelings, and behavior. Typically, teachers assist the child's journey to self-regulation by first co-regulating with them.

Sensitivity (non-resilience): a child's feelings which can be easily hurt. Resilience is attainable and may take a more active co-regulation journey with the teacher or peers. Some children have high autonomic nervous system reactivity scores that places them in a more sensitive attitude in social contexts. These children tend to be more reactive, hypervigilant, and anxious. Often referred to as "orchidial." These learners, when actively engaged, can solve the class for the teacher.

Sensory Information: information processing starts with input from the sensory organs (eyes, ears, hands, tongue, skin, nose etc.), which transform physical stimuli such as touch, heat, sound waves, or photons of light into electrochemical signals. In the classroom, too much sensory input may be responsible for introducing cognitive overload and causing children to react and become disruptive or disengaged.

Serotonin: a neurotransmitter that aids learning and memory formation. Serotonin enhances the neuron's electrical impulse, creating enduring memory. This neurotransmitter is especially active in transmitting impulses between nerve cells, and contributing to well-being and happiness.

Small Motor Skills: activities that require the use of the small muscles of the hands. Mastery is important in early childhood development of many motor skills for normal daily functions. Children need to practice and become proficient in the smaller muscles of the hand in order to hold a pencil, write letters and numbers, and accomplish many other functional skills, like tying a shoe and buttoning a coat.

Social Emotional Learning: thoughts and attitudes that help children align with social norms that drive their maturity. Focus on SEL allows children to build skills and develop healthy identities, manage emotions, achieve personal and collective goals, feel and show empathy for others, establish and maintain supportive relationships, and make responsible and caring decisions.

Somatosensory Cortex: a brain structure that plays a critical role in processing incoming sensory information. It contributes to the integration of sensory and motor signals necessary for skilled movement. In the classroom, teachers can give children practice to play in this space by asking the child to "shut your eyes and identify the object" game. For example, hold an orange behind their back and identify the object based on its texture, temperature, and shape.

Stratification: the (often harmful) classification of children into labeled groups. Even when teachers make their best efforts to shield children from comparisons, they tend to stratify themselves based on labels they hear in school – labels like "Free and Reduced", "Gifted", "IEP", "Special Ed" and so on. Children who are sensitive to comparisons and competitive practices will be damaged emotionally by the labels and subsequent stratification, and this can have a big impact on their life trajectories.

Susceptibility to Social Context: being influenced or potentially harmed by your social environment. All children are susceptible to social context. In schools, social context can be in the classroom, the hallway, the cafeteria, the playing field, and elsewhere. Some children who display natural resilience will survive and thrive in any social setting, but less resilient and more sensitive children might be overwhelmed, afraid, or even terrified of most school social contexts.

Synaptic Connections: chemical transmissions at a junction between two nerve cells. Information from one neuron flows to another neuron across a synapse. Connections typically form between the end of one neuron and a dendrite on another. The connection consists of: i) a presynaptic ending that contains neurotransmitters mitochondria and other cell organelles; ii) a postsynaptic ending that contains receptor sites for neurotransmitters; iii) a synaptic cleft or space between the presynaptic and postsynaptic endings. Excitatory synaptic transmission happens when glutamate, the excitatory neurotransmitter, activates receptors on the postsynaptic neuron. With synaptic connections, brain cells form neural circuits that support sensory, motor, and cognitive skills and that ultimately regulate all behavior.

Synesthesia: a neurological phenomenon in which stimulation of one sensory or cognitive pathway leads to automatic, involuntary experiences in a second sensory or cognitive pathway. In the classroom, the typical synesthete may not know they are synesthetes and assume that their very visible difference, with respect to other children, marks them as being dumb.

T

Tabula Rasa: literally meaning "blank slate," this term refers to the principle espoused by some early philosophers and educators (e.g. John Locke, B F Skinner) idea that the infant is born with no innate capacity —a blank slate that is awaiting input from the environment. Today, we accept that children are born with innate capacity for grammar, language and much more.

Tactile: hands-on activities connected with the sense of touch. In whole-brain teaching activities, the sense of touch is very powerful for the child to make sense of the environment. In each brain there is a strip of cortex which is responsible for processing sensory information from the body (touch, pain, temperature) called the somatosensory cortex. A large part of this "strip" is allocated specifically to processing sensory information from the hands. In addition, the cerebellum fine-tunes motor activities, especially the fine movement of fingers of children who are learning to write or manipulate blocks.

Teach to the Orchid: teachers who solve the orchid child, typically solve the class. When we equate compliance with learning, that decision tends to leave a lot of potential on the table. By orienting our lessons and our predictability, consistency and kindness to orchidial children, we find that all children are able to engage.

Temporal Lobe: in front of the Occipital Lobe, the temporal lobe is associated with auditory processing and olfaction. It is key to being able to understand meaningful speech, hearing and selective listening – all attributes that are vital to learning.

Thalamus: a brain structure that acts as the body's relay station. Information from the senses (except smell) must be processed through the thalamus before being sent to the brain's cerebral cortex for interpretation. The thalamus also plays a role in sleep, wakefulness, consciousness, learning and memory.

Token Economies: a system of bribery for positive behavior reinforcement. A token is given as a reward for a target behavior and the tokens can be exchanged for something the student might want.

U

Universal Design for Learning (UDL): a set of principles to guide the design of learning environments that are accessible and effective for all people. This model claims to deliver inclusive instruction of general education and special education students, allowing general education students access to multiple ways of learning and creating a greater sense of belonging for students with special needs. Teachers use UDL to normalize useful structures in the classroom and reduce stress. At the same time, this method can increase cognitive capacity of not only the student who has an accommodation (IEP), but for any student who might benefit from a more concrete type structure.

Unexpected Behavior: in classrooms, teachers sometimes refer to disruptive and aggressive behavior as unexpected behavior. In reality, given the stressors associated with traditional two-dimensional learning systems, that behavior should be very expected.

Unlimited Potential: every child has a brain that can process 30 billion bits of information per second. And, with its 1000 trillion molecules, it is one of the most complex objects in the universe. So, even though at times it might be difficult to project that a child has unlimited potential, they do have extraordinary capacity, but are constrained by other factors, especially by processing speed and by the limitations of working memory.

Uncover Instead of Cover: traditional learning systems were focused on covering topics via scope and sequence. In a cognitive learning space where the focus is on architecting a child's brain so that they can achieve their true potential, teachers view learning through the lens of uncovering information so that children have opportunities to co-create the learning environment. For instance, in a Dick & Carey model, the instructional designer presents material that flows into terminal objectives by covering topics from a long list.

V

Visual Cortex: located in the brain's occipital lobe (back of the head), the visual cortex processes visual information by recognizing and locating objects. This is the pathway through which conscious visual perception takes place.

Visuospatial Sketchpad: ability to temporarily hold visual and spatial information in working memory. For instance, where you accidentally left your phone and where to go to retrieve it. Working memory is a higher-order process that provides cognitive space for the temporary storage and manipulation of verbal, visual and spatial information. Visual Spatial processing is typically associated with the right hemisphere and includes working memory and executive frontal lobe attentional control mechanisms.

Volitional: a choice, or a decision made, an act of choosing to do something as a result of your own will. In the classroom, the faculty by which a child decides upon and commits to a particular course of action, especially when this occurs without direct external influence.

W

Wernicke's Area: named after the German neurologist Carl Wernicke, a region in the temporal lobe of the brain that contains motor neurons involved in the comprehension of written and spoken language. It is intricately linked with Broca's area which is involved with the production of language. It is located in one of the temporal gyri in the dominant cerebral hemisphere – left for 95% of right-handed people and 70% of left-handed people. Damage to Wernicke's area results in fluent aphasia.

White Matter Structures: myelinated nerve fibers that connect different regions of the brain. The white matter appears white because they take on the color of myelin—the insulation material that covers the nerve fibers. Myelin acts as an insulator, increasing the speed of transmission of all nerve signals.

Whole Brain: refers to activities or teaching methods that use all aspects of the brain (visual, auditory, movement, etc.). Learning systems that are designed to engage all students are more successful when the teacher understands a whole brain approach. When teachers and students are aware of their cerebellum, two hemispheres and four lobes, together with the associated functional specializations, then learning can be more fun, more meaningful and more engaging.

Wilt: following a blooming plant analogy, children who are sensitive to social context may languish and decline, instead of bloom and blossom. As in the plant world, by changing the environment and not the plant, adjusting pH, amount of water, sunlight and so on, the plant can be nudged to bloom, blossom, and flourish. When we do not change the wilting child, but instead introduce adjustments to the learning environment, a child too can bloom, blossom and flourish.

Working Memory: the small amount of information that can be held in the mind in a particular moment for cognitive tasks. Working memory also governs one's ability to retain and manipulate distinct pieces of information over short periods of time.

Z

Zero Tolerance: school discipline policies that are based on progressive, punitive, exclusionary practice that mandate predetermined consequences for behavior, regardless of context or rationale. Outcomes typically involve in-school and out-of-school suspension or expulsion, and are perceived by many to reinforce a child's less than optimal life trajectory that includes a pipeline to prison, poverty, homelessness and suicide.

Tiger Schmiger Series Author

Dr. Kieran O'Mahony is the founder of the Institute for Connecting Neuroscience with Teaching and Learning, an educational non-profit in the State of Washington that facilitates teacher Professional Development for twenty-first century learners.

His award-winning writing ignites learning, inspires teachers and engages children in a subject arena that is both meaningful for lifelong learning, and human potential.

Kieran lives in Seattle, WA, with his children – three boys and a girl, and a black lab puppy. His love of the outdoors includes sailing, high-altitude mountaineering, surfing and kayaking.

"Mental models about how our brains function and how we learn, informs and empowers our innate capacity for change agency. I study the intersection of teaching and neuroscience in a practical collaboration that introduces relevant neuro-knowledge, which profoundly impacts adolescent learning and potential. Areas of expertise include learning sciences, how people learn and neuroscience substrates to many of the daily challenges that impact learning (e.g., stress, attention, working memory, cognition, plasticity). The primary locus of intervention is with administrators and principals where change that is meaningful and practical has high impact for teachers, students, and parents — delicately balanced three-legged stool of learning. Using in situ institutes and professional learning community (PLC) meetings, I co-create with teachers a Mind, Brain, Education (MBE) learning environment that cross-fertilizes domain knowledge with neuro-scientific research applied to learning, developmental psychology for adolescent learning, and practical applications of learning sciences in the field."

Translation of meaningful neuro-informed research delivers pedagogic models that offer nuanced insights to classroom management, content exposition, engagement, and unintended consequences like labeling and stratification, by establishing novel and innovative approaches to educational environments—formal and informal. This work is accomplished through incorporating theories of action and methods that align neuroscience with how the brain works and how people (especially children) learn (HPL), within existing systems and constraints and within a framework of adaptive expertise (AE).

Dr. Kieran is a prolific writer, text book author and speaker. As a renowned expert in an emergent field of learning sciences in cognitive neuroscience he is in high demand as keynote speaker in schools, colleges and educational conferences. In addition, his work has deep meaning for adult learning spaces, where corporate culture, talent development and human resources are aligned with his educative and groundbreaking research findings. Today's workplace is in profound change - legacies of post-pandemic (i) overt intentional distancing, and (ii) covert unintended consequences of intrinsic out-of-office autonomy, mastery and purpose. His 'theory into practice' workshops revitalizes workplace learning by improving professional outcomes and mental health in corporate settings. In Dr. Kieran's world, he looks for opportunities to co-create blended school and workplace learning environments to electrify human spirit and advance sapiens sapiens potential.

Index

3 Cognitive R's – 83

A

Academic Standards – 60

Acting Out – 20

Active Avoidance – 10, 90

Active Learning – 141

ADHD – 72

Aerobic Exercise – 129

Affirmations – 25, 103

Agency – 8, 13, 24, 29, 58, 95, 97

Aggressive – 40–41, 82, 130, 135

Amygdala – 20, 30–31, 33–35, 41, 50, 54–55, 61, 64, 70, 91, 100–101, 130–132, 140–141

Anchor – 39, 108–109, 144

Anticipation – 20, 107, 142

Anxiety – 50–51, 74, 93, 106, 145

Anyone, anyone – 26

Appetite – 15, 22, 66, 78–79, 83, 124, 139–140, 144

Aptitude – 15, 22, 78–79, 83, 124, 139–140

Architect – 47, 78, 88, 104, 119

Assignment wrong – 16

Assimilation – 84

At Risk – 26, 83, 98

Attachment – 16, 98, 105, 143

Attention – 3, 20, 24, 26, 40, 43, 60, 64–65, 70, 82, 85, 89, 98, 104, 121, 126–127, 139–140

Auditory – 20, 30, 89, 130

Authentic Struggle – 94

Autism – 72

Automaticity – 71, 74, 86, 92, 113, 125, 128

Autonomic Nervous System Reactivity – 18, 36, 52, 100, 123, 140

Aversive – 66, 74

B

Basal Ganglia – 31

Behavior – 22, 30, 34, 36, 40–42, 48, 50, 52, 54, 61, 71, 74, 78, 83, 91, 100, 104–106, 117–118, 130–131, 134, 140–144

Behavioral Plans – 36

Beliefs – 4, 10, 16, 20, 68, 84, 102, 132

Bell Curve – 18

Belly Breathe – 15, 75

Better or Worse – 21

Biological Parent – 116

Body Language – 5, 20, 50, 57, 64, 70, 100–101, 132

Boredom – 76–77

Bounce Back – 14–15, 18, 64, 100, 122

Brain-Derived Neurotrophic Factor – 129

Breathe – 5, 30–31, 35, 38, 41, 53–54, 57, 73, 75, 87, 100, 123, 131

C

Cat and Mouse – 66

Catastrophize – 38

Child-Centric – 60, 76, 78–79, 89, 97

Choice – 12, 17, 20–21, 24, 28, 42, 66, 113, 130, 135

Chunking – 113, 115, 121, 123

Circuits – 40, 65, 72, 75, 94, 99, 106, 109–110, 124–125, 129

Classroom Management – 36

Clean Slate – 84

Closure – 84

Co-regulation – 39, 143

Cognition – 11, 21–23, 31, 35, 55, 57, 61, 63, 75, 83, 89, 96–97, 99, 104, 109, 112–113, 115, 118, 121, 124–125, 139, 144

Cognitive Load – 23, 63, 104, 112–113, 115, 118, 124

Cognitive Rehearsal – 11, 35, 96–97, 109, 121, 124–125, 144

Comfort Zone – 58, 94

Communication – 41, 71, 73, 83, 104, 106, 117, 134, 145

Compare and Contrast – 38, 93

Competition – 29, 31, 36, 58–60, 83, 86, 99, 101, 118, 132

Compliance – 58, 70, 78, 82, 118, 171

Concentration – 58, 107

Concrete – 8–9, 11, 13, 15, 21, 23, 53, 122

Consistent – 5, 27, 29, 43, 51, 67, 77–79, 105, 119, 129–130, 133, 135, 143–145

Consistent Caring Adults – 77, 79

Consolidate – 25, 96, 139–141, 144

Contagion – 30

Contagious – 8, 32–34, 50, 53, 74, 82, 103

Content-centric – 78

Continuum – 8–9, 11, 13–15, 17, 19, 21, 23–24, 39, 100, 116, 123

Contribute – 8, 20, 38, 46–47, 49, 53, 58, 60, 72, 88–89, 93, 95, 98–99, 104, 120–121, 125, 141, 144

Correction – 16, 18, 29, 75, 85, 102, 116, 132

Cortisol – 52, 71, 74, 106–107

Cramming for a Test – 92

Critical Thinking – 66, 83, 88, 91, 104

Culture – 49, 51, 71, 79, 116, 118

Curiosity – 37, 77, 141

Curious – 30, 35, 67, 71, 77, 82, 85, 89, 142

Currency of Learning – 97

D

Dandelinic – 42

De-escalate – 34–35, 57, 142

Decentering – 75, 144

Default Mode – 76

Dendrites – 96

Destiny – 25, 139

Detention – 36, 66, 90, 98

Discipline – 34, 36, 60, 82

Discomfort – 94

Disengaging – 20, 67, 140

Disequilibrium – 83–85, 121

Disruptive – 34, 36, 40–42, 67, 74, 82, 98, 130

Diversity – 72, 118, 123

Dopamine – 33, 37, 61, 66–67, 71, 74, 107, 144

Dyscalculia – 72

Dysfunction – 70

Dysgraphia – 72

Dyslexia – 72

E

Early Learning – 98

Effort – 11, 14, 16–17, 22–23, 25, 29, 53, 68, 79, 86, 94, 105, 125, 143

Emotion – 20, 27, 35, 38–39, 51, 53, 58, 65, 78–79, 96, 116, 122, 139–140

Emotional Brain – 142–143, 145

Emotional Setback – 122

Empathy – 57, 144

Engagement – 20, 24, 31, 46–47, 57–60, 65, 72, 74–75, 77–78, 89, 98, 101, 119, 129–130, 132–134, 141–145

Episodic – 65, 128

Equality of Opportunity – 95

Equity – 77, 95, 139

Evolution – 51

Executive Function – 141, 144

Expected Behavior – 48

F

Facilitator – 20, 29, 33, 63, 86, 91, 93, 99, 110, 127, 144

Fail – 12, 16, 22, 28, 36, 42, 66, 68, 71, 78, 92, 103, 107, 115, 139

Failure to Succeed – 116

Fairness – 105

Fallible – 128

Fasciculus – 27

Fawn – 20, 87, 105, 132, 142

Fear – 35, 43, 49-50, 74, 93, 95, 101-102, 114, 117, 133

Feedback – 18-19, 59, 61, 85, 91, 132-133

Fight – 20, 41, 87, 105-106, 132, 142

Filter – 16, 38, 90

Fire Together – 88, 96, 110

Fixed – 8-9

Flight – 20, 87, 105-106, 132, 142

Flow – 51, 75, 93

Focus – 16, 18, 23, 27, 35, 37, 43, 53, 58-61, 64, 66, 69-70, 74, 76, 78, 86-87, 89, 102, 104, 107-109, 115, 118, 120-121, 126-128, 139, 143

Fraud – 114

Freeze – 20, 52, 87, 105, 132, 142

Friendships – 59, 98, 107, 116

Fruitless – 22

Fun – 17, 19, 29, 31, 36-37, 43, 47-48, 53, 59, 63, 65, 71, 74, 82, 85, 92, 97, 99, 101, 105, 107, 115, 120-121, 124, 129, 131-133

G

Generate – 47, 53, 58, 72, 79, 89, 93, 95, 99, 104-105, 110, 121, 141, 144

George Miller – 112

Give up Easily – 13, 14, 58, 132

Goal-Directed – 120

Growth – 8-9, 114, 158, 162, 165

H

Habituate – 10, 158-159

Hardwired – 5, 50-51, 59, 79, 82, 99

Healthy Emotional Bonds – 79

Helpless – 14, 24, 86, 105, 116

Herbert Simon – 112

High Risk – 83, 98

High-Stakes Testing – 118

Hijack – 16, 20, 30, 33-35, 41, 50, 54-55, 61, 70, 91, 100-101, 130-131, 140

Hindbrain – 12, 20, 30

Hippocampus – 31, 65, 129, 141

Homo Sapiens – 46, 112, 142

Hyperactive – 20, 30, 130

Hypersensitive – 20

I

IDK – 87

Implicit Memory – 128

Imposter Syndrome – 16, 114

Inclusive – 63, 95, 99, 101, 133

Inhibit – 8, 31, 74, 120, 130, 143-144

Initial Thoughts – 83, 87

Innate Ability – 99

Intelligence – 9-11, 16, 19, 24, 88

Intentionality – 68, 86-87, 89, 108

Intrinsic Motivation – 17, 53, 101, 104, 113, 120

Isolation – 64, 70, 83, 105, 127

Iteration – 27, 33, 87, 125

J

Jewelry – 54-55

Judgment – 28, 66, 76, 86, 105, 143-144

K

Kind – 26-27, 29-30, 51-52, 142-145

L

Labeling – 12, 18, 36, 39-40, 72, 83, 98, 134

Lagging – 115

Laminate – 13, 15, 17

Less Resilient – 21, 43, 52, 105, 122-123

Limbic Emotional Brain – 143

Lived Experience – 68

Logic – 14, 55, 106, 130

M

Make Visible – 11, 49, 109, 144

Malleable – 10, 24, 46, 69, 73, 116, 128

Mastery – 13, 15, 17, 25, 29, 33, 53, 66, 68-69, 73, 86-87, 89, 99, 101, 104, 113, 115, 121, 129, 133, 135, 143-144

Me Here Now – 59, 65, 76-77, 85, 89-91, 93, 95, 108-109, 144

Meaning-making – 30, 85

Mediated Practice – 85

Memory – 10, 18, 21, 23, 27-28, 56-57, 62, 65, 85, 91-92, 96, 106, 108-113, 121, 128-129, 134, 139, 141, 144-145

Mental Models – 4-5, 14, 19, 35, 39, 61, 70, 84-85, 97, 100, 123, 125, 134-135

Metacognition – 66, 75, 92, 143

Miller's Law – 21, 28-29, 108

Mindset – 5, 8-9, 11-14, 17, 19-25, 34, 66, 68-69, 82, 88, 104-105, 114, 116-117, 130, 140, 144

Mirror Neurons – 41, 54, 57, 131

Misconceptions – 84-85

Mistakes – 18-19, 33, 66, 82, 85, 94, 99, 125, 127, 129, 132, 142

Model – 4-5, 13-15, 17, 19, 22-23, 27, 35, 39, 60-61, 70, 77, 79, 83-85, 97, 100, 118, 121, 123, 125, 130, 133-135, 140, 143

Mood – 57, 103, 144

Myelination – 11, 15, 22, 24, 35, 46, 61, 72-73, 82, 86, 88, 94, 96, 99, 109-110, 115, 124-126, 129, 132, 135, 141-142

N

Negative Criticism – 13, 18

Negative Spiral – 5, 38, 74, 122

Nervous System – 18, 36, 52, 100, 116, 122-123, 140, 145

Neural Lens – 34, 82-83, 98, 110

Neural Plasticity – 11, 22, 69, 72, 139

Neuro-diverse – 72, 164

Neurobiological – 5, 18, 59, 116

Neuron – 24-25, 35, 40-41, 46-47, 54, 57, 86, 88, 94, 96, 102, 106, 110-111, 119, 125, 129, 131

Neurotransmitters – 66, 106-107, 121, 125, 141, 143-144

Norepinephrine – 107, 144

Norm – 30, 51, 87, 115

Not present – 56, 74

Nuanced – 38, 144

O

Olfactory – 30

One-size-fits-all – 18

Oppositional Behavior – 130

Orchidial – 42

Original Thinking – 86-87, 92

Overwhelmed – 14, 21, 28-29, 39, 67-68, 74, 139

Oxytocin – 33, 37, 53, 61, 63, 66, 71, 107, 115, 143-144

P

Perseverance – 16

Persistence – 14-15, 20, 26, 42, 52-53, 58, 84-85, 88, 106, 114, 116, 142

Personality – 49, 58, 114

Personalized Learning – 83

Phenotype – 122

Phonological Loop – 33, 39, 47, 66, 99, 128-129

Piaget – 23, 121

Plasticity – 9, 11, 22, 69, 72, 88, 121, 139

Plateau Early – 22

Potential – 11, 22–26, 36, 67–68, 82, 112, 134–135, 139

Powerlessness – 116

Practice Makes Permanent – 85

Precocious – 82

Preconceptions – 84

Predictable – 5, 27, 29, 43, 51, 67, 105, 129, 133, 144

Prediction – 86–87, 91, 144

Preparation for Future Learning – 92

Primal – 30, 57, 64, 118, 132, 142–145

Principal's Office – 54, 98, 141

Prior Knowledge – 83–84, 91

Procedural Memory – 128

Progress over Competition – 59

Public Shaming – 26, 36–37, 64, 140

Punishment – 36–37, 42, 53, 59–60, 68, 76, 99, 104–105, 109, 126, 132, 140–142

Purpose – 13, 15, 17, 28, 53, 58, 72, 85, 89, 99, 101, 104, 113, 115, 129, 143

Q

Questions – 26–27, 87–88, 90–91

R

Reason – 22, 46, 68, 72, 83–84, 107, 131, 142–144

Recall – 65, 79, 92, 96, 110, 128, 132, 141

Red Marks – 16, 59, 61, 102, 114, 116, 132–133

Red Zone – 13, 15, 17, 19, 21–22, 86

Regulate – 31, 38, 55, 100, 130, 143–144

Regurgitating – 92, 139

Relate – 57, 65, 76, 94, 108, 142–144

Relationships – 31, 36, 43, 47, 49, 67–68, 77, 79, 116, 120, 144

Reminder – 16, 83, 116, 128, 132, 141

Report Out – 77, 93, 95

Resilience – 14–15, 18, 50, 100, 116, 122–123

Retention – 128

Reticular Activating System – 14, 16, 29, 84, 86, 102, 114, 132, 134

Revert to Default – 84

Rewards – 25, 31, 36, 42, 53, 59–60, 64, 66, 68, 103–105, 109, 140–141

Rewiring – 94

Risk – 12, 26, 46, 58, 94

Rote Memory – 92

S

Sapiens – 46, 99, 112, 142, 145

Scaffolding Questions – 87–88, 91

Schema – 108, 121, 142, 144

Scribe – 93

Self-Efficacy – 14, 83, 89

Self-Esteem – 38, 114, 145

Self-Evaluation – 87

Self-Fulfilling Prophecy – 14

Self-Regulation – 39–41, 122, 130, 142–143

Self-Talk – 14–15, 25, 86

Semantic – 128

Sense of Belonging – 14, 31, 37, 53, 58–59, 63, 65, 89, 107, 109, 120, 143

Sensory Information – 20, 30, 51, 64, 110, 113, 120–121, 132

Separation Anxiety – 50

Serotonin – 33, 37, 53, 61, 101, 106–107, 143–144

Serotonin Transporter Gene – 101

Shame – 26–27, 36–37, 64, 83, 140

Short-Term Memory – 128, 134

Single-Task – 87

Sisyphus – 132

Skinner – 10

Sleep – 3–4, 41, 65, 67, 96, 101, 111, 122, 141

Small-Motor Skills – 89

Smart – 12, 114

Smell – 20, 30, 51, 89, 120

Social Context – 5, 20, 43, 59, 100-101, 103, 116-117, 122, 130

Social-Evaluative Threat – 132

Spines – 96, 153

Spiral – 5, 14, 38, 74-75, 87, 114, 122

Stratification – 36

Stressors – 50-52, 67, 74, 106, 131, 135, 142

Stuck Mentality – 17

Success of Others – 13, 20-23, 95

Surprise – 30, 91, 105, 126

Surprising – 91, 93

Survival – 12, 27, 30, 47, 50-51, 58, 86, 105-106, 119, 132, 142-144

Susceptibility – 59, 117

Sweaty Palms – 55

Synapse – 97

T

Tabula Rasa – 84

Tactile Chart – 15

Talent – 10-11, 19, 24, 63, 67, 114

Teach to the Orchid – 29

Test – 70, 92, 139

Thalamus – 30

Threat – 37, 42, 51-53, 82, 87, 101, 140, 147

Three Questions – 27

Tiered System – 98

Time Keeper – 93

Token Economies – 36, 60, 68, 140

Transition – 48, 51, 108

Triggering – 20, 32, 131, 147

U

Uncover – 16, 70

Unexpected Behavior – 48

Unique Brain – 126

V

Visual Thesaurus – 38

Visual-Spatial Sketchpad – 132

Vocabulary – 13, 15, 19, 22, 24, 35, 38-39, 61, 69, 71, 96-97, 100, 123, 125-126, 131-134, 140

W

Wernicke's Area – 99, 129

White Matter – 19, 22, 46-47, 64, 69, 88, 96, 98-99, 104, 109-111, 115, 124-127, 129, 132, 139, 141, 143

Whole Brain – 75, 89, 119

Wire Together – 88, 96

Working Memory – 21, 23, 27, 56-57, 62, 91, 106, 108-109, 111-113, 121, 128, 139, 144-145

Wrong Answer – 18, 33, 89, 141

Z

Zero Tolerance – 34, 42

www.ingramcontent.com/pod-product-compliance
Lightning Source LLC
Chambersburg PA
CBHW081355290426
44110CB00018B/2384